A Troubled Heart

A TROUBLED HEART

DAVID L. BROWN

FOXWARE PUBLISHING LLC

LAS CRUCES, NEW MEXICO

A Troubled Heart

Copyright © 2019 by David L. Brown.

Published by Foxware Publishing LLC, 1156 Cave Springs Trail, Las Cruces, NM 88011.

All rights reserved, including the right to reproduce this book, or portions thereof, in any form. Except for brief quotations in books, articles, and critical reviews, no part of this text may be reproduced, transmitted, downloaded, decompiled, reverse engineered, or stored in or introduced into any information storage and retrieval system, in any form or by any means, whether electronic or mechanical, without the express written permission of the author, except as provided by USA copyright law. The scanning, uploading, and distribution of this book via the Internet or via any other means without the permission of the publisher is illegal and punishable by law. Please purchase only authorized electronic editions and do not participate in or encourage electronic piracy of copyrighted materials. The publisher does not have any control over and does not assume any responsibility for author or third-party websites or their content.

Scripture quotations are taken from the Holy Bible, New International Version®, NIV®. Copyright © 1973, 1978, 1984, 2011 by Biblica, Inc.™ Used by permission of Zondervan. All rights reserved worldwide. www.zondervan.com The "NIV" and "New International Version" are trade-marks registered in the United States Patent and Trademark Office by Biblica, Inc.™

Cataloging Information:

Dewey Decimal Classification 220.7
Printed in the United States of America.
10 9 8 7 6 5 4 3 2 1 0

To

My Family

"Begin at the beginning," the King said, very gravely, "and go on till you come to the end: then stop."

LEWIS CARROLL, ALICE IN WONDERLAND

Contents

Acknowlegements	xi
Prologue	xiii
Chapter 1 In the Beginning	1
Chapter 2 John the Baptist	3
Chapter 3 John Denies Being the Messiah	7
Chapter 4 The First Apostles	13
Chapter 5 Jesus Turns Water Into Wine	15
Chapter 6 Jesus Clears the Temple Courts	17
Chapter 7 Jesus Teaches Nicodemus	21
Chapter 8 John Testifies Again About Jesus	27
Chapter 9 The Samaritan Woman	29
Chapter 10 Jesus Heals an Official's Son	35
Chapter 11 A Healing at the Pool	37
Chapter 12 The Authority of the Son	41
Chapter 13 Jesus Feeds the Five Thousand	47
Chapter 14 Jesus the Bread of Life	51
Chapter 15 Jesus Walks on the Water	55
Chapter 16 Many Disciples Desert Jesus	57
Chapter 17 The Festival of Tabernacles	59
Chapter 18 Jesus the Light of the World	63
Chapter 19 Dispute Over Jesus' Testimony	67
Chapter 20 Dispute Over Who Jesus Is	69
Chapter 21 Sin and Slavery	71
Chapter 22 Jesus' Claims About Himself	73
Chapter 23 Jesus Heals a Man Born Blind	75
Chapter 24 The Good Shepherd	79
Chapter 25 The Death of Lazarus	83
Chapter 26 The Plot to Kill Jesus	87
Chapter 27 Jesus Anointed at Bethany	89
Chapter 28 Riding a Donkey	91
Chapter 29 Jesus Predicts His Death	93
Chapter 30 Belief and Unbelief	97
Chapter 31 Jesus Washes His Disciples' Feet	101
Chapter 32 Jesus Comforts His Disciples	107
Chapter 33 The Vine and the Branches	113
Chapter 34 The Promise of the Advocate	119
Chapter 35 Jesus Prays to be Glorified	125
Chapter 36 Jesus Arrested	129
Chapter 37 Jesus Crucified	137
Chapter 38 The Empty Tomb	145
Chapter 39 Miraculous Catch of Fish	153
About the Author	159

ACKNOWLEDGEMENTS

First I want to thank my pastor, David Borrows. He was the pastor of First Baptist Church Las Cruces during the time I was writing this and was a real source of information and inspiration. His preaching is second to none in Bible-backed messages that he delivers with few notes, no pulpit, and seemingly perfect recall. He doesn't get sidetracked and holds my attention like few pastors ever have. Second is my friend Jim McPherson who read and discussed with me some doctrinal points. We didn't agree on some of the timing around the crucifixion but we did agree 100% on the main issue. That is Christ's resurrection and shed blood is the sacrifice for our sins. He offers this to us and ALL who believe will have eternal life. I also want to thank my wife. She was the first one to read it through and her advice was short and to the point. She said I needed to re-edit it myself. She was right. Last, but not least, I want to say thanks to Harry James Fox. He is more than my mentor. He got me from writing the book to getting it published, which was a burden off of my shoulders. He also read and made comments on style and presentation which are a help. He has published several books which can be found on http://wwwfoxwarepublishing.com.

PROLOGUE

The desire to write this book was initiated by a sermon I heard my pastor preach; I believe in Aug. of 2017. I don't really remember the topic but I remember him saying that he read the book of John more than any other book. He was answering a general question about how one should go about studying the Bible.

He had 3 points:

1. There is really never anything new. God's imprint has always been in our hearts and it will always be there and he has never altered the moral code at any time or for anyone.

2. The complete Bible is relevant to what we need to know about God. It should all be read at some point. It is all God's word and we should recognize it as that and don't add to or take away.

3. It is not all equally important. Reading it from cover to cover so that you can say you did isn't the most successful approach to using it. It is a book to be used not just read. He said he read John I believe more than any other and then Acts and Romans and the other Gospels. He said he reads here by far the most. He preaches the gospel and this is where it is found. He does read Paul but reads the Gospels more. People are tempted to think Paul wrote the most of the New Testament but this isn't true. His books and chapters are short compared the Gospels and if Luke wrote Luke and Acts, he obviously wrote the most. John, however, is the very heart of the gospel ("gospel" meaning the good news about Jesus Christ) and therefore the core of the Bible. John is more about the Spiritual Jesus. The other gospels are more about the physical Jesus.

These thoughts started me on a new course. I have begun to read it for the purpose of hiding it my heart and letting it guide me, instruct me change me, thrill me. New thoughts and recollections seem to come each time and I thought it was time to write some of them down even if I am the only person that may ever see them.

I wondered where I should start and remembered probably the most intimate thing that has ever happened to me with the Scripture. I was in the hospital laying on a gurney in preparation to enter an operating room for a hernia repair. Not really all that serious a thing. A nurse had been in my room the night before however doing her job of instructing me that I was going under general anesthetic and there was some risk that I would never wake up. I had already received the first of the anesthesia injections. I wasn't unconscious yet. I was just lying there by the nurse's station looking at the lights. The question came—will I ever see these lights again? I don't remember ever memorizing John 14:1-4 but these words drifted into my mind.

John 14:1 Do not let your hearts be troubled. You believe in God; believe also in me.

2 My Father's house has many mansions; if that were not so, would I have told you that I am going there to prepare a place for you?

3 And if I go and prepare a place for you, I will come back and take you to be with me that you also may be where I am.

4 You know the way to the place where I am going."

I started my study there and worked to the end. I have often avoided this latter part of all the Gospels because it is so sad and gruesome. But it is absolutely the core of the Bible. I then finished by studying the first 13 chapters. For the purpose of writing, however, I will start at Chapter 1 and finish at 21.

In comparing the Bible to an apple tree. I think I heard this from my pastor. The fruit would be the New Testament and John would be the very core. We will study the core, which contains the seed. The seed and only the seed have the things in it that are necessary to reproduce the tree so in that light it is the most important part. Now, however, we need to see the whole picture and the next is the apple itself. In my analogy I see this as the Gospels and John being the first if you try to rank by importance. I am going to use John to do this but will make an attempt to do as complete a job as I can by inserting other Gospel verses and other Scripture where it seems relevant to me. Most of these I will look up and include. I don't intend to use any other reference material. I do use quotes from my pastor quite often and will note that. My firm belief is that the Bible and the Holy Spirit are the key places you find God speaking to you. Don't misunderstand. He does use other methods and people quite often. In my case this has been true, particularly when I wasn't walking on the path he wanted. He would do something to get my attention. Preachers are also biblical and important. Any time you introduce people, however, there is room for doubt. Keep this in mind as you read this. My words could and should be questioned. My desire is to take a journey down this path of knowledge that is the Gospel (GOOD NEWS) of Christ. If you don't want to continue reading this and just want to open your Bible and start wherever God leads you, then do that. You are not making a mistake and I won't know it but if I did, I would not take offence. Also understand that this cannot ever be considered as complete. As John himself says there isn't enough paper on earth to contain the whole.

Chapter 1

†

In the Beginning

John 1: 1-5

John 1:1 *In the beginning was the Word, and the Word was with God, and the Word was God. 2 He was with God in the beginning. 3 Through him all things were made; without him nothing was made that has been made. 4 In him was life, and that life was the light of all mankind."5 The light shines in the darkness, and the darkness has not overcome it.*

I remember as a child wondering why the word "Word" was used here. I didn't immediately make the connection that John was talking about Jesus. Had I continued reading I would have found the answer. John1: 6-34 provides the answer. Jesus has ALL the attributes of God and he completely and totally participated in the creation. His special function was to bring life and light. This part of God was not named "Jesus" until he became flesh and dwelt among us. The name Jesus first appears in verse 17. The doctrine of the trinity is a New Testament doctrine. As often happens this passage puts life before light and we humans want to trust our own rational and think that light was necessary before life as we know it could start. What John is writing is Spiritual however. The Spirit of God and therefore Jesus has always existed and physical light was created. Word now becomes meaningful in that He is Gods message to us. He brings light and life. God, including Word, changes some dirt into something that can recognize God. Gen. 2:6-7. He gave us a mind that could understand words. He gave us the knowledge that God exists and he is available to us. Nothing will ever be able to take that away from us. Verse 5 says Light overcomes the darkness and it always will. Word is the origin of life and light. THE LIGHT OF THE WORLD IS JESUS. PRAISE GOD, PRAISE GOD, PRAISE GOD!

Chapter 2
†

John the Baptist
John 1: 6-18

John 1:6 *There was a man sent from God whose name was John. 7 He came as a witness to testify concerning that light, so that through him all might believe. 8 He himself was not the light; he came only as a witness to the light. 9 The true light that gives light to everyone was coming into the world. 10 He was in the world, and though the world was made through him, the world did not recognize him. 11 He came to that which was his own, but his own did not receive him. 12 Yet to all who did receive him, to those who believed in his name, he gave the right to become the children of God—13 born not of natural descent, nor of human decision or a husband's will, but born of God.*

14 The Word became flesh and made his dwelling among us. We have seen his glory, the glory of the one and only Son, who came from the Father, full of grace and truth.

15 (John testified concerning him. He cried out, saying, "This is the one I spoke about when I said, 'He who comes after me has surpassed me because he was before me.'") 16 Out of his fullness we have all received grace in place of grace already given. 17 For the law was given through Moses; grace and truth came through Jesus Christ. 18 No one has ever seen God, but the one and only Son, who is himself God and is in closest relationship with the Father, has made him known."

Next in John we see John the Baptist. He is called that because his trademark is baptism to demonstrate repentance. John doesn't mess around.

Verse 6 says where John the Baptist came from and what his assigned task is. He is from God. His job is to bear witness concerning who Jesus is. Pretty much the same as ours. John's target audience was to the Jews who knew the Mosaic Law but not necessarily them only. Our audience by our commission is the whole earth. John the Baptist was more unique than we are however. I recommend you stop here and read these references to see what the Bible says about John the Baptist. Here is the major portion of them. Isaiah 40:3, Mal.4:5-6, Matt.3:1-12, Matt.4:12, Matt.11:2-19, Matt. 14:1-12, Mk.1:2-8, Mk. 6:14-29, Mk.9:11-13, LK. 1:5-24, LK.3:15-18, , LK.7:18-35, LK.9:7-9, (Jn.1:6-35, 3:27-30, 5:33-36. These are included in this writing)

In verse 9-14 John writes a short but pointed discourse about who Jesus is and how the world has reacted to him. He also points out clearly that this is a spiritual thing – not born of a husband's will but of God. John 4:24 says God is a Spirit. They that worship him worship him in Spirit and in truth.

God sent John to tell who the Messiah is. He gave this sign to John – which the Spirit would descend on the Messiah in the form of a dove and John would see. I don't know if other people saw this or not. No other record indicates that anyone else saw it or would have understood the significance if they did. Because of this sign then John knew that Jesus was the Messiah. He tells everyone that this is the case. (After some thought my true feeling is that believers saw this and unbelievers didn't. Believers being people who have believed or are going to believe that Jesus is the Messiah. It is a true sign of the Messiah and these are not hidden from believers.) John also understands that the mission of the Messiah is to bring light into the world. He understood and testified that Jesus did not have an earthly father and that believing Jesus (his 2nd cousin) was the Messiah was the way to get to heaven. It is the way to attain eternal life. John and his writing can say it better than I can. The Word became flesh and dwelt among us. He is called Jesus. As he says by believing in him, we become the sons of God. To this very day that is completely true. Time going by doesn't change anything where God is concerned.

Verses 15 through 18 state that a new way to God is here. Following the law that God gave through Moses is going to be replaced by the new law of grace and truth through Christ. He also stresses that Christ is the only one who has seen God. He is the Son who came down from God. (This is stated by Christ about himself several times in John) This is important because this is a qualification of the Messiah—to be a messenger from God. An additional thought I have had is that this means the entity in the Garden of Eden must have been the Son because Adam saw him before he sinned. He saw and was judged by him after he sinned. I believe He started bearing our sins right then.

The significance of Jesus being baptized becomes clearer also. Jesus himself is a prophet and his main prophecy is that he is going to die and rise again. His baptism is a physical demonstration of what the future holds for him. Jesus says in Matthew 3 that he is doing this to fulfill all righteousness. In other words, in order to be right with God he needed to be baptized. God wanted it so Jesus did it. Whether we understand this completely now or not is pretty insignificant. He marks this Baptism, descending of the Holy Spirit as a dove and the voice of God saying, "this is my beloved son in whom I am well pleased" as the beginning of God's very orchestrated demonstration of who Jesus is. John the Baptist is a main character in this and his main line is " BEHOLD THE MESSIAH".

Another thing to explore is Matt. 11:14 where Jesus says:

14 And if you are willing to accept it, he is the Elijah who was to come.

This prophesy is in Mal. 4:5-6. These are the last 2 verses in the Old Testament. It says:

Mal.4:5-6 See, I will send the prophet Elijah to you before that great and awful day of the Lord comes. He will turn the hearts of the parents to their children and the hearts of the children to their parents or I will strike the land with total destruction.

As I read through Elijah's history (I Kings 17-19) looking for why he and John the Baptist are alike and how they are different than other prophets I see:

1. We only see a portion of each of their lives, which is spent, along the Jordon River and in the wilderness to the East.

2. Israel had degenerated to a nation that completely turned their back on God in both cases. In Elijah's time it was the worship of Baal. In John's time it was worship of works and legalism.

3. God talked directly to both of them. There are some comparisons that can be made between the sacrifice that Elijah made the sacrifice that Jesus made which John prophesied about.

4. They both lead very separated lives. They both knew what God was doing but had some doubts.

In Mat.11: 2-6 we hear Jesus talking about John the Baptist. He is a prophet; however, he is more than just a prophet. He is the voice of one crying in the wilderness, "Make straight the path of the Messiah." In the ranking of men, then, John the Baptist is the very highest. Jesus expresses a very beautiful thing, (Matt. 11: 11 *"Truly I tell you, among those born of women there has not risen anyone greater than John the Baptist; yet whoever is least in the kingdom of heaven is greater than he."*)

He starts his teachings about the Kingdom of heaven. When we get to heaven ranking will not play a role. We will all be the same amount of clean because he washes us all with the same blood and that is his blood.

Prophesies about the Messiah: Nm. 24:15-19, Ps. 22:1, Is. 53, Ps. 45

Chapter 3
†

John Denies Being the Messiah
John 1: 19-34

John 1:19 *Now this was John's testimony when the Jewish leaders in Jerusalem sent priests and Levites to ask him who he was. 20 He did not fail to confess, but confessed freely, "I am not the Messiah."*

21 They asked him, "Then who are you? Are you Elijah?"

He said, "I am not."

"Are you the Prophet?"

He answered, "No."

22 Finally they said, "Who are you? Give us an answer to take back to those who sent us. What do you say about yourself?"

23 John replied in the words of Isaiah the prophet, "I am the voice of one calling in the wilderness, 'Make straight the way for the Lord.'"

24 Now the Pharisees who had been sent 25 questioned him, "Why then do you baptize if you are not the Messiah, nor Elijah, nor the Prophet?"

26 "I baptize with water," John replied, "but among you stands one you do not know. 27 He is the one who comes after me, the straps of whose sandals I am not worthy to untie."

28 This all happened at Bethany on the other side of the Jordan, where John was baptizing

29 The next day John saw Jesus coming toward him and said, "Look, the Lamb of God, who takes away the sin of the world! 30 This is the one I meant when I said, 'A man who comes after me has surpassed me because he was before me.' 31 I myself did not know him, but the reason I came baptizing with water was that he might be revealed to Israel."

32 Then John gave this testimony: "I saw the Spirit come down from heaven as a dove and remain on him. 33 And I myself did not know him, but the one who sent me to baptize with water told me, 'The man on whom you see the Spirit come down and remain is the one who will baptize with the Holy Spirit.' 34 I have seen and I testify that this is God's Chosen One."

In John 1:19 thru 34, John the Baptist makes several enlightening statements. He has been preaching for a while about this. He doesn't say how long but it could have been for 2 or 3 years. Enough time so the people standing around listening have heard it long enough to know the message i.e. *the Messiah is coming!! I am not worthy to tie his shoes.* Long enough to have some followers. He makes sure they understand that he is not the Messiah. I have an opinion here; the reason John's life was ended the way and at the time it was served the purpose of keeping the belief that he was the Messiah from spreading. His method of death was not a cruel one. He also emphasizes that he isn't the other prophet or Elijah. He has his own specific prophecy to fulfill and that to be: *the voice of one crying in the wilderness (Is.40:3) make straight the way of the Lord.*

John the Baptist states that the reason he is baptizing with water in vs.31 is done so that Jesus might be revealed to Israel (as the Messiah). In the other Gospels we see John the Baptist saying that Jesus should be baptizing him instead of Jesus being baptized by John the Baptist but Jesus points out that this is a God thing so they will do it as instructed by God. Again, it is not clear to me why this is but this much is clear—it was God's well-orchestrated plan of showing Israel and the rest of the world that **Jesus is the Messiah**. My present lack of understanding doesn't change what it is. There is also little doubt that John the Baptist's baptism was a complete immersion thing. Each place that it is being done there is water sufficient for that purpose. John also makes it clear that he knows that this one that is coming is an entity that existed before him. He says that in verse 15. He knows that he is God in the flesh and that He will baptize with the Holy Spirit. John the Baptist's preaching and first encounter with Jesus happened close to Bethany (east), which is up close to the Sea of Galilee. There must have been an easy way to get across the Jordon there. I suppose they could have gone up to the lake and crossed in boats. He doesn't talk about Jesus' baptism till after the fact in the next verses.

There are a few things about John the Baptist that I don't completely understand. His baptism for repentance is one. He was baptizing people who were publicly demonstrating and confessing repentance of the thing they recognized as sin in their lives. They were being baptized because they wanted an outward show of an inward change. *If we confess our sins, He is faithful and just to forgive our sins and cleans us from all unrighteousness* (1Jn 1:9) is just as true for these people as it is after Christ's death and it is the same today. It also has to do with repentance because when he was asked what they should do his answer was in short, stop sinning. The word repentance means to turn away from. There just doesn't seem to be any president for the baptisms. Jesus and John and the Old Testament and the New Testament all teach the same thing about sin. In order to be cleansed of it what we have to do is repent of it. Turn away from it. Concerning John's baptism John says in verse 31 that he has been given specific instruction to baptize with water so that the Messiah can be revealed to Israel. In John 1:33 he says the one who told him to baptize with water also told him how he would know the Messiah when he saw him. He said that the Spirit in the form of a dove would come and sit on Him. In reading the other accounts of this it is entirely possible it happened more than one time. It happened when Jesus was baptized. (Matt.3: 16, Mk.1:9, Lk.3:22) In Jn.1:31-34 John tells about seeing the Spirit descending on Jesus but doesn't tell about Jesus baptism. The Spirit descending could have happened more than one time but my feeling is that it only happened one time and He was only baptized one time. The same principle applies as with our baptism. We only need to do it one time. Our salvation only happens one time. Jesus' death and resurrection only happens one time. We either believe in Jesus as our savior or we don't. That is what determines our eternal fate. THIS IS THE ONE SINGLE MOST IMPORTANT THING IN THE BIBLE.

Verses 1:29-31 contains John's main description of who Jesus is. His first statement is that he is the Lamb of God who takes away the sins of the world. I don't think that many of the people who heard this statement understood at all what John was talking about. I am not even sure John the Baptist did. He understood it partly that is obvious but did he understand that this Lamb had to die? John the Baptist was faithful to his commission however and this is what God sent him to the earth to tell. He then repeats the fact that Jesus existed before John the Baptist did. John wrote the first 6 verses and included them first so that we can understand what John the Baptist understood and is stating here. Jesus has always existed. He predates all of humanity and all of creation. He predates the sun and moon and earth and sky and stars. He along with God and the Holy Spirit predate everything. They have always existed. John the Baptist then tells about the dove. He says that God talked to him. He told him to baptize with water. He said the reason is so that Jesus would be revealed to the Israelites. John the Baptist said that he did not recognize Jesus as the Messiah but then the thing that God said would happen did happen. A dove came and sat on him and remained on him. The picture I have in my mind is that Jesus came to John the Baptist and asked to be baptized by him. As he did this dove came and sat on Jesus' shoulder. They had the conversation about who should be baptizing. They went down into the river and John the Baptist baptized Jesus. God's voice from heaven said, "This is my beloved Son in whom I am well pleased". The dove stayed on Jesus' shoulder during this whole procedure. John clearly states that GOD told him this would happen and that this was the sign that Jesus is the Messiah. He also understood the dove was the Spirit of God not just any ordinary dove. He understood because God told him and he listened and didn't doubt, at least at this point. He also says that he didn't know Jesus. I'm not sure what he meant exactly but my best guess is that he knew Jesus was his mother's sister's daughter's son but he did not know he was the Messiah. He also certainly may have meant that he had never met Jesus and therefore didn't recognize him. I would imagine however that he did know that he existed. You might also remember from what you have read that John's parents knew that their son would play a part in the coming of the Messiah. John the Baptist would have been told of his own miraculous birth and the message that the angel Gabriel brought to his father. He would have known of Mary's visit with his mother I would think. This doesn't really matter however. The Messiah was (and is) a Message and demonstration directly from God. (one of the things John the Baptist has in common with Elijah, i.e. God spoke directly to him.) It is also interesting that John th Baptist already knew that the Holy Spirit would be the connection between us and God the Son and God the Father. Baptism is a demonstration of our desire to be a recipient of this Spirit. The dove was a demonstration of this Spirit so we see then at Jesus' baptism God the Father speaks, the Spirit is there in the form of a dove, and Jesus the Savior of the world is baptized. God is complete here but then I don't believe that God ever leaves himself out. Jesus and God are only separated one time and that is when Jesus is hanging on the cross.

I also have this thought about Jesus' baptism: He did not need to repent of sin that he had committed. He was not guilty of any. He did bear the sins of the entire human race however. He did die for those sins and was buried and rose again the third day and that is what this baptism foretells.

Chapter 4
†
The First Apostles
John 1: 35-51

John 1:35 *The next day John was there again with two of his disciples. 36 When he saw Jesus passing by, he said, "Look, the Lamb of God!"*

37 When the two disciples heard him say this, they followed Jesus. 38 Turning around, Jesus saw them following and asked, "What do you want?"

They said, "Rabbi" (which means "Teacher"), "where are you staying?"

39 "Come," he replied, "and you will see."

So they went and saw where he was staying, and they spent that day with him. It was about four in the afternoon.

40 Andrew, Simon Peter's brother, was one of the two who heard what John had said and who had followed Jesus. 41 The first thing Andrew did was to find his brother Simon and tell him, "We have found the Messiah" (that is, the Christ). 42 And he brought him to Jesus".

Jesus looked at him and said, "You are Simon son of John. You will be called Cephas" (which, when translated, is Peter).

Jesus Calls Philip and Nathanael

43 The next day Jesus decided to leave for Galilee. Finding Philip, he said to him, "Follow me."

44 Philip, like Andrew and Peter, was from the town of Bethsaida. 45 Philip found Nathanael and told him, "We have found the one Moses wrote about in the Law, and about whom the prophets also wrote—Jesus of Nazareth, the son of Joseph."

46 "Nazareth! Can anything good come from there?" Nathanael asked.

"Come and see," said Philip.

47 When Jesus saw Nathanael approaching, he said of him, "Here truly is an Israelite in whom there is no deceit."

48 "How do you know me?" Nathanael asked.

Jesus answered, "I saw you while you were still under the fig tree before Philip called you."

49 Then Nathanael declared, "Rabbi, you are the Son of God; you are the king of Israel."

50 Jesus said, "You believe because I told you I saw you under the fig tree. You will see greater things than that." 51 He then added, "Very truly I tell you, you will see heaven open, and the angels of God ascending and descending on the Son of Man."

A day passes here. We see Andrew and John follow Jesus from this point. From what is said later I am sure John the Baptist encouraged them to do this. John isn't named but here again as you read it becomes the only choice. In a short time here, Jesus gets 5 of the apostles. Andrew, Simon, John, Philip and Nathanial. Jesus changes Simon's name to Peter. In thinking about why Jesus did this my feeling is that he knew what the future held for Peter and what he would use Peter to do and say. Two statements come to mind. One is in John 6:67-68 when Jesus asks: *Are you going to desert me too?* and Peter says, "Where would we go. You are the Messiah". Another is in Matt 16:16 when Jesus asks: *But who do you think that I am?* and Peter says, "You are the Messiah, the Son of the living God". Jesus says in Matt. 16:17 that this is directly from God. We can see Peter being prepared to be the foundation preacher for the new church. (Acts 2:14-41). In verse 49 we hear Nathanial declare that Jesus is the Son of God and the king of Israel, which indicates that he believes him to be the Messiah. I am not sure about Jesus' answer because I am not sure when the ascending and descending incident or incidents happened. Jesus said it would, however, so I believe that it did. It probably also indicates that Nathanial lacked some Spiritual discernment about the Spiritual Messiah. He did not yet understand that Jesus is going to be the ultimate sacrifice for the sins of the world.

Chapter 5
†

Jesus Turns Water Into Wine

John 2: 1-12

John 2:1 *On the third day a wedding took place at Cana in Galilee. Jesus' mother was there, 2 and Jesus and his disciples had also been invited to the wedding. 3 When the wine was gone, Jesus' mother said to him, "They have no more wine."*

4"Woman, why do you involve me?" Jesus replied. "My hour has not yet come."

5 His mother said to the servants, "Do whatever he tells you."

6 Nearby stood six stone water jars, the kind used by the Jews for ceremonial washing, each holding from twenty to thirty gallons.

7 Jesus said to the servants "Fill the jars with water"; so they filled them to the brim.

8 Then he told them, "Now draw some out and take it to the master of the banquet They did so, 9 and the master of the banquet tasted the water that had been turned into wine. He did not realize where it had come from, though the servants who had drawn the water knew. Then he called the bridegroom aside 10 and said, "Everyone brings out the choice wine first and then the cheaper wine after the guests have had too much to drink; but you have saved the best till now."

11 What Jesus did here in Cana of Galilee was the first of the signs through which he revealed his glory; and his disciples believed in him.

12 After this he went down to Capernaum with his mother and brothers and his disciples. There they stayed for a few days.

This is the first of the miracles that lots of scholars say are the proof miracles i.e. the ones Jesus does to prove who he is and the ones he is referring to when he says in several places if you don't believe me then believe what I do. There are 7 of these miracles if you don't count the 153 fish in chapter 21 and 8 if you do. There are many more miracles if you count everything Jesus does that other people can't do without his help. Jesus does, however, somewhat refer to these himself and he says he is doing what he has seen the Father do. This first one, however, seems a little out of step and Jesus says this. He rebukes his mom a little bit because he says he isn't quite ready to start this demonstration of what he can do. Mary's response indicates however that she has already seen his ability to do very miraculous things. All of his miracles primarily show who He is. I am sure it did impress those first 5 apostles. When you think about the quantity it makes you smile. It must have been a large wedding if what he did is any indication. The amount was between 120 gallons and 180 gallons. The barrels we are used to looking at hold 55 gallons. There is about 6 average bottles of wine in each gallon. That is 900 or so bottles of wine. They didn't use bottles but just a way to get an idea of the size of the wedding. Jesus always made more than was used, however. We don't know. It was a miracle that commanded attention.

Chapter 6
†
Jesus Clears the Temple Courts
John 2: 13-25

John 2:13 *When it was almost time for the Jewish Passover, Jesus went up to Jerusalem. 14 In the temple courts he found people selling cattle, sheep and doves, and others sitting at tables exchanging money. 15 So he made a whip out of cords, and drove all from the temple courts, both sheep and cattle; he scattered the coins of the moneychangers and overturned their tables. 16 To those who sold doves he said, "Get these out of here! Stop turning my Father's house into a market!" 17 His disciples remembered that it is written: "Zeal for your house will consume me."*

18 The Jews then responded to him, "What sign can you show us to prove your authority to do all this?"

19 Jesus answered them, "Destroy this temple, and I will raise it again in three days."

20 They replied, "It has taken forty-six years to build this temple, and you are going to raise it in three days?"

21 But the temple he had spoken of was his body.

22 After he was raised from the dead, his disciples recalled what he had said. Then they believed the scripture and the words that Jesus had spoken.

23 Now while he was in Jerusalem at the Passover Festival, many people saw the signs he was performing and believed in his name.

24 But Jesus would not entrust himself to them, for he knew all people.

25 He did not need any testimony about mankind, for he knew what was in each person."

These incidents in the temple, when Jesus takes a cord and makes a whip out of it and rampages through the temple court, are recorded early in John. Matthew put it right after Jesus riding into Jerusalem on a donkey, which is the Sunday before the Friday crucifixion day. I think John puts it here because he is interested in the Spiritual meaning of the incident rather than any physical thing it may have caused. They both relate it to the Passover. He is saying loud and clear – I AM GOD. This is my house and you treat it like you own it. You treat it like you should make money by trading and charging tax and selling sacrifices. It is supposed to be clean and it smells and looks like a barnyard. You are supposed to worship me here and not do business. He also fulfills several scriptures along the way.

I want to break right here and investigate when each of the disciples came into the group of 12. We see the first 5 already. Luke 5 indicates that this is probably 6 already because John has a brother, James and Jesus enlists him at the same time. In Luke 5:27-31 we see Jesus call Levi a tax collector.

The Twelve Apostles

Luke 6:12 One of those days Jesus went out to a mountainside to pray, and spent the night praying to God. 13 When morning came, he called his disciples to him and chose twelve of them, whom he also designated apostles: 14 Simon (whom he named Peter), his brother Andrew, James, John, Philip, Bartholomew, 15 Matthew, Thomas, James son of Alphaeus, Simon who was called the Zealot, 16 Judas son of James, and Judas Iscariot, who became a traitor."

It seems possible to me then that by the time Jesus got to Jerusalem and clears the courts he already had selected his 12 apostles. You can imagine the effect this had on them. He was actually more in charge of what was allowed in the temple than the priests were. I wondered if any of them pitched in and helped him. Luke indicates that he selected the 12 but there were a lot more than 12 following him. Later most turn away but not all. I suspect also that this incident sort of solidified the idea in their mind that Jesus was going to take over and establish his authority physically. I think they probably thought he was going to rule and he was going to rule from this temple. (His Father's house). He said something that they really didn't understand. Tear this down and I will rebuild it in 3 days. As John points out, He was talking about his body and he did that by coming back to life on the 3rd day. I also believe that this action and statement had great Spiritual significance. Christianity that Christ established has as its cornerstone the resurrection of Christ – the empty tomb. The mercy seat is no longer the place where God can be found on earth. Earthly temples and altars are no longer of any significance. Animal sacrifices and sacrifices of any kind are no longer required. God himself has made the ultimate sacrifice. There is no substitute. Accepting this sacrifice as a gift from God himself is the one and only way you will ever find yourself in his presence.

John 2:23-25 indicates something that was also new to them. Our relation to him is an individual thing. He sees all of us as individuals. He knows what is in our hearts. For the few of them that were really beginning to understand him they began to understand that he knew what was in their hearts. He knew what was in their mind and he knew that for most of them they really didn't know him nor could he trust them. Religion may be a corporate thing but salvation is not.

Chapter 7
†

Jesus Teaches Nicodemus

John 3: 1-21

John 3:1 *Now there was a Pharisee, a man named Nicodemus who was a member of the Jewish ruling council. 2 He came to Jesus at night and said, "Rabbi, we know that you are a teacher who has come from God. For no one could perform the signs you are doing if God were not with him."*

3 Jesus replied, "Very truly I tell you, no one can see the kingdom of God unless they are born again."

4 "How can someone be born when they are old?" Nicodemus asked. "Surely they cannot enter a second time into their mother's womb to be born!"

5 Jesus answered, "Very truly I tell you, no one can enter the kingdom of God unless they are born of water and the Spirit. 6 Flesh gives birth to flesh, but the Spirit gives birth to spirit. 7 You should not be surprised at my saying, 'you must be born again. 8 The wind blows wherever it pleases. You hear its sound, but you cannot tell where it comes from or where it is going. So it is with everyone born of the Spirit."

9 "How can this be?" Nicodemus asked.

10 "You are Israel's teacher," said Jesus, "and do you not understand these things? 11 Very truly I tell you, we speak of what we know, and we testify to what we have seen, but still you people do not accept our testimony. 12 I have spoken to you of earthly things and you do not believe; how then will you believe if I speak of heavenly things? 13 No one has ever gone into heaven except the one who came from heaven—the Son of Man. 14 Just as Moses lifted up the snake in the wilderness, so the Son of Man must be lifted up, 15 that everyone who believes may have eternal life in him.

John 3:16 For God so loved the world that he gave his one and only Son that whoever believes in him shall not perish but have eternal life.

17 For God did not send his Son into the world to condemn the world, but to save the world through him. 18 Whoever believes in him is not condemned, but whoever does not believe stands condemned already because they have not believed in the name of God's one and only Son. 19 This is the verdict: Light has come into the world, but people loved darkness instead of light because their deeds were evil. 20 Everyone that does evil hates the light, and will not come into the light for fear that their deeds will be exposed. 21 But whoever lives by the truth comes into the light, so that it may be seen plainly that what they have done has been done in the sight of God."

My first comment is we need to be very thankful for Nicodemus. It seems like Jesus isn't very patient with him. I think however without Jesus' firmness with him he may have continued down the track he was on and that was the track of the Pharisees. I am a Pharisee and therefore already one of God's chosen people. I was born a full-blooded Jew. I was schooled as a Jew as a child. I know the law and have lived by it mostly. I have made appropriate sacrifices for the times I failed. I have made sacrifices for times I failed and didn't even know it. I tithe. I give to the poor. Not only that I am a member of the Sanhedrin. Jesus knew who he was. He probably knew all of the members of this council. You would not have had to worry however. He wore a robe that was unique to the group. I—having been in the Army—would know a General when he walked by. I would know his name, his rank, what unit he commanded where he had served if I had kept up with his ribbons. I'm not sure you would have known that much about Nicodemus but he was dressed appropriately for who he was. He was a proud man. If a General came to my house and knocked on the door and wanted a conversation with me I think I could be pretty sure he knew something about me before he walked in the door. He, for instance, could have looked in my file and found out what kind of a soldier I had been. Nicodemus had done a similar thing and he started the conversation that way. He didn't have anything to read but he had been watching and listening. Wouldn't be surprised if he hadn't watched a little of the Temple clearing by Jesus. He didn't say that, however. He said he saw some of the miracles, healings, and things like that. He recognized that the average sorcerer out there could not do these things Jesus was doing. He had also saw Jesus teaching his followers. He had analyzed what he saw and heard and formed a conclusion. His conclusion was a logical one. Jesus was a teacher sent from God. Like so many good conclusions we form he came to it with too few facts and lack of real research. He totally ignored what Jesus said about himself, he totally ignored what John the Baptist said about Jesus and preached about Jesus. He had not met his mom and found out that he was not the average child. More than that, he had never really researched the Messiah. He knew he was foretold but that was about it. He was intent on being obedient to the law but a prime example of missing the essence of the Bible.

Thinking of this in that light, then I guess Jesus was pretty kind to him. He told him the truth in terms he could understand. As is the case most of the time, Jesus was speaking Spiritually and Nicodemus was thinking physically. I think he got the picture in the end because he helped bury Jesus – spared no expense to do it as good as he could. He also tried to some degree to get the Sanhedrin to act in a rational way. Like most groups of men who try this they are too bent on their own status to hear sound judgment.

For us and for Nicodemus the message is clear. A person has to be born 2 times to gain eternal life. One of those births is physical and the other is spiritual. The physical one is no problem. It wasn't our choice. As far as we are concerned, we just came into being. As far as our parents are concerned it isn't a whole lot more than that. Sure, they had a relationship and ideally were married so we have a chance to get started right and learn all the things a kid needs to know about how to live and be kind and good and honest and faithful. When you are my age you are saying to yourself 'bout 10 more years and my lights are going out. In fact, they are getting kind of dim already. And really that is it physically. Sure, some people get rich, some live in poverty, some live in a free country, some live in broken homes, some work hard, some don't work at all, some are sick, some are completely healthy their whole life, some are naturally happy, some are naturally unhappy. Some are on the earth a short time and some a long time like me. But what is a long time? 95 years? Compared to eternity that is nothing. I have empathy for Nicodemus. It is kind of like Jesus is talking a brand-new language. He is saying things that are completely new to Nicodemus. He indicates that they shouldn't be but they are. His comparison is to the wind. We cannot see wind yet everything else tells us it is there. God is similar. We can't see him, touch him, yet he is there. Verses 17 and 18 are very important to understanding this. We are already in trouble. We are already dead. Just like a dead man can do nothing to get back alive again so we can do no work to get spiritual life. We can't regain it because we never had it in the first place. Verse 14 is the lead-in verse. I suspect Nicodemus didn't understand it completely. It probably was the most shocking thing he had ever heard. I do think that he understood Jesus was talking about himself when he says "The Son of Man". He certainly knew the snake in the wilderness story. It is possible he had this burning question in his mind, "Is he telling me that he is going to be crucified?"

AND THEN WE HAVE 3:16. The burning question for all of us is what does he mean when he says, "Believeth in Him"? What is it that we have to believe? That he was born of a virgin. He had an earthly mom and a heavenly Dad ; that he lived a sinless life even though he was tempted the same as us; that he died a physical and a Spiritual death; that he came back to life on the third day; this was necessary to provide the blood sacrifice for the remission of our sins. Believing in him means that you accept him for what he is. My pastor points out and I also believe that the only thing you actually have to believe is that after being dead he was brought back to life. He preaches a complete series titled "What do you do with the empty tomb?" Jesus spends the last 3 years of his earthly life proving who he is. He does it front of a lot of people. Many wrote about it. God inspired many people to write and has by a miracle itself made it for us to read. We all can see. There really is no doubt that it is true. He does it very specifically. Nicodemus himself will participate in front of and with these 12 chosen men. A few of the things only they see. If you believe he immediately becomes your savior. You understand you are born (spiritually). You become his Spiritual child. Like a child you need a lot of attention at first (and really your whole life). He provides it however. What kind of a child you turn out to be is somewhat up to you but he definitely prefers good ones. He promises the Holy Spirit. Have everlasting life means exactly what it says. You are his child for the rest of eternity starting right then. You cannot be unborn spiritually any more than you can be unborn physically. Spiritual life lasts forever. Where you spend it is determined by believing or not believing in him. It isn't something you can change your mind about. If you say to yourself, "Well, I will give it a try." you haven't believed. Here are some additional verses that will help. These come from the Children's program our church uses:

Rev.4:8 *Holy Holy Holy is the Lord God almighty; who was and is and is to come.*

Romans 5:8 *But God demonstrates his love for us in this that while we were yet sinners Christ died for us.*

1 Cor.15:3-4 *"For what I received I passed on to you as of first importance : that Christ died for our sins according to the Scriptures, that he was buried, that he was raised on the third day according to the Scriptures"*

Acts 16:31 *"Believe in the Lord Jesus, and you will be saved"*

Romans 3:23 *"for all have sinned and fall short of the glory of God,"*

Romans 6:23 *For the wages of sin is death but the gift of God is eternal life through Jesus Christ our Lord.*

Johnn 3:19-21 point out what the problem is for most people. It isn't that they don't understand. They can see the light and they realize that if they accept it they have to turn away from darkness. They have this false concept that they can do their own biding in the dark and not be seen. We all have this desire to be in charge ourselves but it will not work. Satan tells us we can't succeed. That is a bald-faced lie. We can succeed. ALL WE HAVE TO DO IS BELIEVE. Reading this chapter over 2 or 3 or 10 times is better than reading what I have written. Let it soak in. Let the light shine in. Accept the truth for what it is.

Chapter 8
†
John Testifies Again About Jesus
John 3: 22-36

John 3:22 *After this, Jesus and his disciples went out into the Judean countryside, where he spent some time with them, and baptized. 23 Now John also was baptizing at Aenon near Salim, because there was plenty of water, and people were coming and being baptized. 24 (This was before John was put in prison.) 25 An argument developed between some of John's disciples and a certain Jew over the matter of ceremonial washing. 26 They came to John and said to him, "Rabbi, that man who was with you on the other side of the Jordan—the one you testified about—look, he is baptizing, and everyone is going to him."*

27 To this John replied, "A person can receive only what is given them from heaven. 28 You yourselves can testify that I said, 'I am not the Messiah but am sent ahead of him.' 29 The bride belongs to the bridegroom. The friend who attends the bridegroom waits and listens for him, and is full of joy when he hears the bridegroom's voice. That joy is mine, and it is now complete. 30 He must become greater. I must become less." "

31 The one who comes from above is above all; the one who is from the earth belongs to the earth, and speaks as one from the earth. The one who comes from heaven is above all. 32 He testifies to what he has seen and heard, but no one accepts his testimony. 33 Whoever has accepted it has certified that God is truthful. 34 For the one whom God has sent speaks the words of God, for God gives the Spirit without limit. 35 The Father loves the Son and has placed everything in his hands. 36 Whoever believes in the Son has eternal life, but whoever rejects the Son will not see life, for God's wrath remains on them."

John 3:22-36 is John the Baptist stating his affirming dissertation. John at this point had seen the Dove, had heard God speak, had seen Jesus do several miracles and heard about others he had done. He knew who he was because God had revealed that to him in the wilderness. He said to the religious leaders "I am the voice of one crying in the wilderness "Make straight the way of the Lord" so he realized he was the one prophesied about in the Old Testament. I have heard other people and even here in John start listing the proofs that Jesus gives for who he is. Some list 7 miracles because the leave off the 153 fish. In the last part of this writing I will list many more than 7. I select the ones I list by them being something that only Jesus and God can do. This John the Baptist dissertation is certainly a proof of who Jesus is. John also states that he is full of joy because he knows that Jesus is the Messiah. If you think of ranking them in importance, certainly Jesus himself is by far on the top. I think then that John the Baptist would probably be next. John himself might be next and Peter would stand beside him. Jesus himself, however, teaches that there is no rank in heaven. The 7 miracles that are chosen do, however, seem to have the specific purpose of pointing out characteristics of Jesus.

Chapter 9
†
A Samaritan Woman
John 4: 1-42

John 4:1 *Now Jesus learned that the Pharisees had heard that he was gaining and baptizing more disciples than John— 2 although in fact it was not Jesus who baptized, but his disciples. 3 So he left Judea and went back once more to Galilee.*

4 Now he had to go through Samaria. 5 So he came to a town in Samaria called Sychar, near the plot of ground Jacob had given to his son Joseph. 6 Jacob's well was there, and Jesus, tired as he was from the journey, sat down by the well. It was about noon.

7 When a Samaritan woman came to draw water, Jesus said to her, "Will you give me a drink?" 8 (His disciples had gone into the town to buy food.)

9 The Samaritan woman said to him, "You are a Jew and I am a Samaritan woman. How can you ask me for a drink?" (For Jews do not associate with Samaritan.)

10 Jesus answered her, "If you knew the gift of God and who it is that asks you for a drink, you would have asked him and He would have given you living water".

11 "Sir," the woman said, "you have nothing to draw with and the well is deep. Where can you get this living water? 12 Are you greater than our father Jacob, who gave us the well and drank from it himself, as did also his sons and his livestock?"

13 Jesus answered, "Everyone who drinks this water will be thirsty again, 14 but whoever drinks the water I give them will never thirst. Indeed, the water I give them will become in them a spring of water welling up to eternal life."

15 The woman said to him, "Sir, give me this water so that I won't get thirsty and have to keep coming here to draw water."

16 He told her, "Go, call your husband and come back."

17 "I have no husband," she replied.

Jesus said to her, "You are right when you say you have no husband. 18 The fact is, you have had five husbands, and the man you now have is not your husband. What you have just said is quite true."

19 "Sir," the woman said, "I can see that you are a prophet. 20 Our ancestors worshiped on this mountain, but you Jews claim that the place where we must worship is in Jerusalem." "

21 "Woman," Jesus replied, "believe me, a time is coming when you will worship the Father neither on this mountain nor in Jerusalem. 22 You Samaritans worship what you do not know; we worship what we do know, for salvation is from the Jews. 23 Yet a time is coming and has now come when the true worshipers will worship the Father in the Spirit and in truth, for they are the kind of worshipers the Father seeks. 24 God is spirit, and his worshipers must worship in the Spirit and in truth."

25 The woman said, "I know that Messiah" (called Christ) "is coming. When he comes, he will explain everything to us."

26 Then Jesus declared, "I, the one speaking to you—I am he."

The Disciples Rejoin Jesus

27 Just then his disciples returned and were surprised to find him talking with a woman. But no one asked, "What do you want?" or "Why are you talking with her?"

28 Then, leaving her water jar, the woman went back to the town and said to the people, 29 "Come, see a man who told me everything I ever did. Could this be the Messiah?" 30 They came out of the town and made their way toward him.

31 Meanwhile his disciples urged him, "Rabbi, eat something." "

32 But he said to them, "I have food to eat that you know nothing about."

33 Then his disciples said to each other, "Could someone have brought him food?"

34 "My food," said Jesus, "is to do the will of him who sent me and to finish his work. 35 Don't you have a saying, 'It's still four months until harvest'? I

tell you, open your eyes and look at the fields! They are ripe for harvest. 36 Even now the one who reaps draws a wage and harvests a crop for eternal life, so that the sower and the reaper may be glad together. 37 Thus the saying 'One sows and another reaps' is true. 38 I sent you to reap what you have not worked for. Others have done the hard work, and you have reaped the benefits of their labor."

Many Samaritans Believe

39 Many of the Samaritans from that town believed in him because of the woman's testimony, "He told me everything I ever did." 40 So when the Samaritans came to him, they urged him to stay with them, and he stayed two days. 41 And because of his words many more became believers.

42 They said to the woman, "We no longer believe just because of what you said; now we have heard for ourselves, and we know that this man really is the Savior of the world."

I like this woman. I've heard lots of sermons on this encounter that make this woman seem like a prostitute or at least a woman who can't stay married. Some say that she is out there in the heat of the day so she doesn't have to associate with other women because they look down on her. My feeling however is that I know almost nothing about her culture. I would guess, however, that everyone in this village got water from that well and carried it in a pot back to their house. Having talked to a few missionaries who lived in this situation this is a major task. You went and got water when your pot got empty. There was only one person there because that is what Jesus wanted. (Spiritual thing)

Jesus himself is the first to break custom. He speaks to her. There must have been something there to sit on because he is sitting down. He asked her for a drink of water. I believe that if he had been anything except a Jewish man this would not have been out of line. People do need to drink and carrying water a long way if your only transportation is your feet isn't nearly as good as using the water along the way. I actually think that may be why he stayed at the well. (not a very good thought—he stayed at the well to talk to this woman) Her answer when he asked for a drink shows in my opinion a strong character. I think the more common thing would have been to ignore him and fill her pot and hurry off or give him a drink and not talk to him, or see him sitting there and stay away till he left. It never says that she gave him a drink but I have the feeling she did. Her response indicates a strong, uninhibited personality. Her question basically was, "What has motivated you to step out of your culture and talk to me?" Jesus didn't engage in small talk like we are very prone to do. The most obvious one would have been something to the effect that thirst outranked Judaism when you are really thirsty. There is a good chance also that she had seen the other men and knew that he would get a drink in some manner rather than asking her. His disciples' reaction kind of indicates this. She points out to him what his custom is supposed to be. I suspect she isn't nearly as hung up on custom as she thinks he is. He then starts a spiritual conversation with her. She (as with us most of the time) doesn't immediately recognize this. He tells her about living water and she thinks of being relieved of one of her main tasks—getting water to drink and cook with and wash with, etc. She also wanders obviously how he is going to get this water since he has just violated one of his main rules and that is to talk to her in order to get some for himself. Her question about Jacob I believe is a very honest one. She really wondered if he was saying he was greater, more powerful, more motivated than Jacob. She still hasn't got the Spiritual picture. I believe that the next thing he said was to set up a miracle specifically for her. It had the purpose of getting her on the right track. It pushed her to the knowledge that he was Supernatural. He was not just an ordinary man. In fact, he was a prophet. She asked him a question that indicates she has questions about how to worship. In a short sentence he revealed that he knew her past. Her answer revealed that she was basically an honest person. We immediately jump to the conclusion that having 5 husbands and not being married to the man she presently lived with is SIN spelled with a capital S. We don't know their culture. Pretty sure they did not have a welfare system like we have. Most countries don't. What we know about national leadership in that day and age government did very little to provide for the citizenry. Women in general had to do something to keep from starving to death. Being joined to a man was pretty much a necessity. There are exceptions, I'm sure, but for the most part a woman needed a protector and men in general could have more than one wife and could have other women under his roof that weren't his wife. I have probably spent too much time here. it served Jesus' purpose. It suggests that she has committed the sin of adultery in her past but what he says is that she is not sinning now by saying something that isn't true. She does not let it warp her personality. He takes time to answer her question. Again, you get the feeling that the question is one Jesus wants her to ask because He wanted to answer it. It also seems very like Jesus is controlling this situation because she recognizes him as the Messiah. Truly, this is exactly how it happens with us today. The Holy Spirit leads us just like he led this Samaritan woman. In the end of this conversation Jesus makes 2 declarations.

- 1. God is a Spirit and they that worship him must worship him in Spirit and truth.
- 2. The woman said "I know that the Messiah is coming". Jesus said, "I—the one speaking to you—I am He".

This incident much like John the Baptist is not one of the 7 proofs but yet in my mind like John the Baptist this incident is one of the very main things that helps show who Jesus is.

In the Spiritual realm brothers and sisters hold the same status. Really there is no status. We all have the same need and He provides for that need equally.

Jesus says Salvation is of the Jews. He demonstrates, however, it is for everyone. I have heard that for Jewish people Samaritans were even lower than Gentiles. They were half-breeds. They are kind of like the Mormons. In Mormon belief, the only way you will ever make it all the way to hell is be a Mormon and then turn away from Mormonism. Samaritans had really violated what God had instructed them to do. God had instructed them to kill all the people in the land they possessed but they didn't do that. In fact, they brought them into their society by marrying them. Jew, gentile, half-breed all hold the same status. Really there is no status. We all have the same need and He provides for that need equally.

The woman immediately becomes a witness. This is another thing that makes this woman such a likeable person. She left her pot—probably so the apostles could use it while she was gone and she told everyone she could about who was out at the well. She must have had some status because they believed her enough to go and see and listen. Change started in many of their lives that day.

Chapter 10
†
Jesus Heals an Official's Son
John 4: 43-54

John 4:43 *After the two days he left for Galilee. 44 (Now Jesus himself had pointed out that a prophet has no honor in his own country.) 45 When he arrived in Galilee, the Galileans welcomed him. They had seen all that he had done in Jerusalem at the Passover Festival, for they also had been there.*

46 Once more he visited Cana in Galilee, where he had turned the water into wine. And there was a certain royal official whose son lay sick at Capernaum.

47 When this man heard that Jesus had arrived in Galilee from Judea, he went to him and begged him to come and heal his son, who was close to death.

48 "Unless you people see signs and wonders," Jesus told him, "you will never believe."

49 The royal official said, "Sir, come down before my child dies."

50 "Go," Jesus replied, "your son will live."

The man took Jesus at his word and departed. 51 While he was still on the way, his servants met him with the news that his boy was living.

52 When he inquired as to the "time when his son got better, they said to him, "Yesterday, at one in the afternoon, the fever left him." 53 Then the father realized that this was the exact time at which Jesus had said to him, "Your son will live." So, he and his whole household believed.

54 This was the second sign Jesus performed after coming from Judea to Galilee.

In this section we see the second miracle that John lists as a proof. He says this in verse 54. An official's son was about to die and he had heard that Jesus had made the journey from Judea to Galilee. I don't know how much pride-swallowing he did. He had heard and maybe even seen some of the things that Jesus did and obviously lots of them had to do with healing people of serious defects. We easily understand his misery. His son was about to die. Jesus makes a comment to him that on the surface seems to be a little rude. You people won't believe unless you see signs. What Jesus said, however, was exactly the truth and in reality, much of what he did was to prove who he was because a man could not do them by himself. Jesus states this about himself in chapter 5. He does what he has seen his father do and his father also does it on the Sabbath. This ruler however seemed to have the understanding that if Jesus wanted to do a miracle it didn't matter who he was or whether he necessarily deserved it. He also accepted that physical contact wasn't necessary. A beginning of understanding that Jesus was doing spiritual things not physical. That seems to be the lesson unique to this miracle. Here again, Jesus picked someone who to the Jews didn't believe deserved attention.

Chapter 11
†
The Healing at the Pool
John 5: 1-15

John 5:1 *After Some time later, Jesus went up to Jerusalem for one of the Jewish festivals. 2 Now there is in Jerusalem near the Sheep Gate a pool, which in Aramaic is called Bethesda and which is surrounded by five covered colonnades. 3 Here a great number of disabled people used to lie—the blind, the lame, the paralyzed. 4 From time to time an angle of the Lord would come down and stir up the waters. The first one into the pool after such a disturbance would be cured of whatever disease they had. 5 One who was there had been an invalid for thirty-eight years. 6 When Jesus saw him lying there and learned that he had been in this condition for a long time, he asked him, "Do you want to get well?"*

7 "Sir," the invalid replied, "I have no one to help me into the pool when the water is stirred. While I am trying to get in, someone else goes down ahead of me."

8 Then Jesus said to him, "Get up! Pick up your mat and walk." 9 At once the man was cured; he picked up his mat and walked.

The day on which this took place was a Sabbath, 10 and so the Jewish leaders said to the man who had been healed, "It is the Sabbath; the law forbids you to carry your mat."

11 But he replied, "The man who made me well said to me, 'Pick up your mat and walk.'"

12 So they asked him, "Who is this fellow who told you to pick it up and walk?"

13 The man who was healed had no idea who it was, for Jesus had slipped away into the crowd that was there.

14 Later Jesus found him at the temple and said to him, "See, you are well again. Stop sinning or something worse may happen to you."

15 The man went away and told the Jewish leaders that it was Jesus who had made him well.

Chapter 5 begins with another of the 7 miracles. Some time has gone by. Jesus and his disciples are back down in Jerusalem. There is a pool there close to one of the gates. What I have read leads me to believe that Jerusalem got its water from a viaduct that was built into the city. This pool got its water from there. My modern mind and having owned swimming pool make me wonder about being healed in that day and time by getting into a public pool. This is an interesting pool however. It says that the water in this pool healed people when it moved. It didn't work all the time but when the water moved the first one in was healed. The way it is worded however indicates it had quit working or maybe it had just quit moving very often because it doesn't sound like there is a crowd of sick people there when this happened. There was some however and this one man had been there for a long time. He also had an additional problem. When the water did move, he couldn't get himself in before some less crippled person got in. A sad situation. Jesus speaks directly to the man and asks him if he wants to be healed. This seems to be a strange question to me. Why would the man be here and especially for the long time if he didn't want to be healed? And yet what else could Jesus say that would result in the right conversation. The man didn't come with the answer I probably would have. My answer might have resulted in Jesus healing someone else. The man explains why the pool hasn't worked for him and Jesus heals the man and gives the man some instructions. He was obedient and followed them. The rest of this incident begins John's rendition of one of the main issues the Jews had with Jesus i.e. He didn't follow the Sabbath laws. The question now is why did Jesus do this particular miracle. My feeling is (1) there is a good crowd to see what happened, (2) the man was in a pretty hopeless situation (3) He wanted the issue of meaningless laws brought out. Jesus could very easily told the man to wait till 6:00 PM so he wouldn't be breaking the Sabbath but he didn't do that. In the next section he deals with this (4) He has a very pointed thing to say to the man (I suspect he says it to most of us from time to time). Stop sinning or something worse may happen to you. We think that poor health etc. is just because. My conviction is that a great deal of it is caused by sin—our sin, our parent's sin, our poor laws, etc. Look around. The world in general is sick and getting sicker. Actually, it is all caused by sin generally speaking. Nothing evil comes from God. No sin starts with him. My belief is that Satan is the original sinner so allowing him to have an influence in our lives will definitely cause sin.

Chapter 12

†

The Authority of the Son
John 5: 16-47

John 5:1 *So, because Jesus was doing these things on the Sabbath, the Jewish leaders began to persecute him. 17 In his defense Jesus said to them, "My Father is always at his work to this very day, and I too am working." 18 For this reason they tried all the more to kill him; not only was he breaking the Sabbath, but he was even calling God his own Father, making himself equal with God."*

19 Jesus gave them this answer: "Very truly I tell you, the Son can do nothing by himself; he can do only what he sees his Father doing, because whatever the Father does the Son also does. 20 For the Father loves the Son and shows him all he does. Yes, and he will show him even greater works than these, so that you will be amazed. 21 For just as the Father raises the dead and gives them life, even so the Son gives life to whom he is pleased to give it. 22 Moreover, the Father judges no one, but has entrusted all judgment to the Son, 23 that all may honor the Son just as they honor the Father. Whoever does not honor the Son does not honor the Father, who sent him.

24 "Very truly I tell you, whoever hears my word and believes him who sent me has eternal life and will not be judged but has crossed over from death to life. 25 Very truly I tell you, a time is coming and has now come when the dead will hear the voice of the Son of God and those who hear will live. 26 For as the Father has life in himself, so he has granted the Son also to have life in himself. 27 And he has given him authority to judge because he is the Son of Man.

28 Do not be amazed at this, for a time is coming when all who are in their graves will hear his voice 29 and come out—those who have done what is good will rise to live, and those who have done what is evil will rise to be condemned. 30 By myself I can do nothing; I judge only as I hear, and my judgment is just, for I seek not to please myself but him who sent me.

31 If I testify about myself, my testimony is not true. 32 There is another who testifies in my favor, and I know that his testimony about me is true.

33 You have sent to John and he has testified to the truth. 34 Not that I accept human testimony; but I mention it that you may be saved. 35 John was a lamp that burned and gave light, and you chose for a time to enjoy his light.

36 I have testimony weightier than that of John. For the works that the Father has given me to finish—the very works that I am doing—testify that the Father has sent me. 37 And the Father who sent me has himself testified concerning me. You have never heard his voice nor seen his form, 38 nor does his word dwell in you, for you do not believe the one he sent. 39 You study the Scriptures diligently because you think that in them you have eternal life. These are the very Scriptures that testify about me, 40 yet you refuse to come to me to have life.

41 I do not accept glory from human beings, 42 but I know you. I know that you do not have the love of God in your hearts. 43 I have come in my Father's name, and you do not accept me; but if someone else comes in his own name, you will accept him. 44 How can you believe since you accept glory from one another but do not seek the glory that comes from the only God?

45 But do not think I will accuse you before the Father. Your accuser is Moses, on whom your hopes are set. 46 If you believed Moses, you would believe me, for he wrote about me. 47But since you do not believe what he wrote, how are you going to believe what I say?

John 5:16-45 is basically one of Jesus' dissertations on who he is. He builds it around several amazing statements. The first one I see is "My Father is always at his work to this very day, and I too am working". God works on Sunday. What? Says right there he does. I guess working on Sunday may not be wrong. My personal feeling is that we should set aside a day for rest and dedicated worship time but it doesn't have to be Sunday. We violate this commandment big time most of the time but not by picking the wrong day. After some thought and prayer this cleared up for me. It is the same issue that Jesus always has and that is we think physically and he is thinking, teaching, acting Spiritually. Doing Spiritual work is nourishing. He tells his disciples this at the well. I don't believe healing someone or creating wine or walking on water, creating food etc. caused fatigue in Jesus' body. Whether it did or not is pretty insignificant. Seeking to do good every day is right. The next statement is John 5:19: *"Very truly I tell you, the Son can do nothing by himself; he can do only what he sees his Father doing, because whatever the Father does the Son also does."*

Question: Did God in the Old Testament turn water into wine? He didn't do this exact thing but there are many instances where he provided food and water when there wasn't any. The biggest was feeding the 600,000 Israelites for 40 years in the wilderness. He also provided water. He provided quail. He provided manna in the right amount every day. He fed Elijah and the Shunammite widow. Several others are there. Did God heal anyone – yes. Think of what you have read in the Old Testament. The Syrian general Naaman is an interesting story. Did he walk on the water? Well not exactly—he just moved it out of the way. Point is, God the Father did many, many miracles and he basically did them for exactly the same reason Jesus did the ones he did – to prove who he was. All of God's miracles had a point and so do all of the ones Jesus does.

John 5:24 is next: *"Very truly I tell you, whoever hears my word and believes him who sent me has eternal life and will not be judged but has crossed over from death to life."* This really doesn't need explaining. It is why you need to read these words until you really understand them. Understand that these are God's words directly to you. You say, "David, these words are for everyone." You are right, but you need to personalize them and understand that they can be for everyone and still be very personal. This can be the case because God is completely consistent. There is only one way for you to reach Him and that is through his Son.

John 5:28 *"Do not be amazed at this, for a time is coming when all who are in their graves will hear his voice 5:29 and come out—those who have done what is good will rise to live, and those who have done what is evil will rise to be condemned."* Not only has God raised people from the dead he is going to raise every person that has been created and they will meet justice square in the face. We who are covered with the blood and have our white robes will not be judged here. Our time will be a time of rewards not punishment. Read these verses carefully several times. I tend to skip over them but I should read them over and over till the truth penetrates deeply. These 2 verses and the conversation Jesus had with the thief on the cross lead to an interesting discussion. Are Saints in their graves? My take on it is that Saints are already in a part of heaven called paradise. I am sure there is no waiting or misery of any sort waiting for us on the other side. If you think physically there is a problem because some of the Saints have already been resurrected—the thief being one—and that includes all of the Saints that came out of the grave when Jesus died. If you think Spiritually, then time isn't an issue. Spiritually, salvation is one occurrence and it happened on the cross. Also, I am convinced that time is a physical thing not a Spiritual thing. This spiritual thing can be stretched out over as much physical time as God desires. For every sinner that has ever lived to stand there and be sentenced for all of his wrong deeds is going to take a while. For every Saint to get his rewards is also going to be long – but then we are in eternity where time has a different meaning if it even exists. No time is a difficult concept for me. Some people think that time shall be no more but that is one of those things that you don't find in the bible just the hymnbook. This is a fact, however the new spiritual life he promises us if we believe in him is everlasting. If it is everlasting then I suppose time no longer has any significance. John tells us in Revelation that in the new heaven and the new earth there is no sea. I think that would pretty much eliminate physical life as we know it if this actually means there is no water. What this points out is that we lack a great deal of understanding. Like Paul says in 1 Cor. 13, *Now we see as through a dark glass but then face to face. We shall know even as we also are known.* My best guess is that our Spiritual body will be much more real than our present physical one is. I Just have a vague glimmer of how that is. Some of the things I think about it are: Our memory will be perfect, we will have knowledge that exceeds our earthly experience, i.e. we will know who everyone is, we will run and not grow weary, we will eat for pleasure and not for sustenance, we will not contain any wearing parts, we will be known by everyone there, we will be defined by what we have done to be in God's will, there will be no pain or sorrow. There will be no pecking order, there will be plenty to do and no limit on time to do it and we won't suffer from fatigue in any way. Love will be the controlling emotion and we will do it without reservation. God will be present and visible and communicative and kind the same as he has always been. Nothing will separate us from him ever again. He has prepared a place for each of us and it is right in his house (heaven). It is a BIG place but will take us no definable time to travel around. Kind of like Phillip. We can think about it and be there. We will be like Jesus completely and we see here in these verses that Jesus only does what God does. I don't think we will be creators but we will be able to copy him in every other thing. We can actually do that now. The fruits of the Spirit will rule us in everything. I am sure I have missed something. I suggest you stop and just think about heaven right now. Can you imagine it, do you want to go, and are you ready to go? Do you believe in Jesus? I hope and pray your answer is yes. If your answer is no I beg you, study John (and other places that might lead you in the Bible) and let the Holy Spirit work in your mind and Believe. Accept his gift of Spiritual life.

These also are two verses that you need to be careful and not take them out of this passage and make them stand-alone. If you do you will get to the wrong assumption that you get to heaven by doing good works. If you leave them in context you see that they mean that your works demonstrate what you have believed. Believing in Christ is what provides salvation.

John5:31 needs to be understood correctly. Here again is a verse that needs to be kept in context. "If I testify about myself, my testimony is not true." What Jesus is saying is that he isn't telling them what he is doing. He is telling them what God is doing through him. Here are the rest of the verses:

"32There is another who testifies in my favor, and I know that his testimony about me is true.

33"You have sent to John and he has testified to the truth. 34 Not that I accept human testimony; but I mention it that you may be saved. 35 John was a lamp that burned and gave light, and you chose for a time to enjoy his light.

36 "I have testimony weightier than that of John. For the works that the Father has given me to finish—the very works that I am doing—testify that the Father has sent me. 37And the Father who sent me has himself testified concerning me. You have never heard his voice nor seen his form, 38 nor does his word dwell in you, for you do not believe the one he sent. 39 You study the Scriptures diligently because you think that in them you have eternal life. These are the very Scriptures that testify about me, 40 yet you refuse to come to me to have life.

41 "I do not accept glory from human beings, 42 but I know you. I know that you do not have the love of God in your hearts. 43 I have come in my Father's name, and you do not accept me; but if someone else comes in his own name, you will accept him. 44 How can you believe since you accept glory from one another but do not seek the glory that comes from the only God?

45"But do not think I will accuse you before the Father. Your accuser is Moses, on whom your hopes are set. 46 If you believed Moses, you would believe me, for he wrote about me. 47 But since you do not believe what he wrote, how are you going to believe what I say?"

How do we know who Jesus is? There is John, although Jesus prefers Spiritual witnesses to physical ones. God himself gave John this job. There is God the Father. They (being the unbelievers who are questioning him) don't hear God (physically or Spiritually) but God himself speaks when Jesus is baptized. We learned this when we looked at John the Baptist. There is Jesus himself. We will see this clearly in the next chapter. There are his works. He has done a lot already but we will see some phenomenal ones in the next chapters. He says that these are a witness to who he is. He says this several times. He says it specifically to his disciples in chapter 14. I guess you could have 5 witnesses if you want to include the Scriptures, which include Moses. I wondered about Moses and what Jesus said about him being the judge. After prayer and thinking again I was led back to Spiritual thinking. What I see is Moses standing on a mountain and he has two stone tablets. And on those stones are 10 words. (quoting my pastor on the 10 words) The judgment that everyone faces is based on these 10 words. There is nothing unclear about them but many are blind and cannot see them. What they do is make us all guilty of violating them. The result is death. Life comes through the blood of Jesus. This is the message we will hear many times as we work our way through John.

CHAPTER 13
†
Jesus Feeds the Five Thousand

John 6: 1-15

John 6:1 *Some time after this, Jesus crossed to the far shore of the Sea of Galilee (that is, the Sea of Tiberias), 2 and a great crowd of people followed him because they saw the signs he had performed by healing the sick. 3 Then Jesus went up on a mountainside and sat down with his disciples. 4 The Jewish Passover Festival was near.*

5 When Jesus looked up and saw a great crowd coming toward him, he said to Philip, "Where shall we buy bread for these people to eat?" 6 He asked this only to test him, for he already had in mind what he was going to do.

7 Philip answered him, "It would take more than half a year's wages to buy enough bread for each one to have a bite!"

8 Another of his disciples, Andrew, Simon Peter's brother, spoke up, 9 "Here is a boy with five small barley loaves and two small fish, but how far will they go among so many?"

10 Jesus said, "Have the people sit down." There was plenty of grass in that place, and they sat down (about five thousand men were there). 11 Jesus then took the loaves, gave thanks, and distributed to those who were seated as much as they wanted. He did the same with the fish.

12 When they had all had enough to eat, he said to his disciples, "Gather the pieces that are left over. Let nothing be wasted." 13 So they gathered them and filled twelve baskets with the pieces of the five barley loaves left over by those who had eaten.

14 After the people saw the sign Jesus performed, they began to say, "Surely this is the Prophet who is to come into the world."

15 Jesus, knowing that they intended to come and make him king by force, withdrew again to a mountain by himself."

Chapter 6 begins with a miracle. Again, some time passes and we see Jesus by the Sea of Galilee. It says he went up on the side of a hill. Word got out and a big crowd showed up – 5,000 men. Pretty sure there were women and young people and children there also. There was at least one boy and he had brought his lunch. He had 5 biscuits and 2 small fish. Jesus asks Philip a question and John points out that Jesus already had a plan in mind. When you think of Phillip's direct encounters with Jesus you see a man whose faith isn't very strong. Kind of like most of us. Phillip and Jesus both knew an answer to the question. Their answers were different however. Phillip's answer is, "We can't. We don't have enough money." Jesus' answer was "it's going to take a miracle. But then that is what I do." And he proceeded to do just that. Andrew must have had some idea what might happen because he mentioned this boy with a lunch. I know that I say over and over again to not add or take away from the scripture but here I just have this urge to make something up. It's morning and this boy had been out on the street the day before listening to people talk. Some of them were really excited because they had seen this man called Jesus heal some people. He was the same man they said that made all that wine. He asked his mom if he could go down by the lake where the fishing boats usually came in and see if he could see him and see if he did another miracle. He had heard that several of the men following him were fishermen. I think he was a trustworthy kid because his mom not only let him go she fixed him a lunch. She knew her son and knew he would travel a ways if he had to. This made-up story of mine helps me a little bit because there is a question in my mind. It is why did Jesus take this boy's lunch and turn it into a large quantity. He had the ability to start with nothing. My feeling is that it is a better demonstration of how we find him. We have to be willing to bring ourselves. He isn't going save us if we don't ask. The bible teaches this very clearly Matt. 7:7 and many others in both the old and new testaments. As I mentioned before, God fed people in the Old Testament and Jesus copies him here. Like it says in Ps 23, the crowd's collective cup ran over. They had 12 baskets-full left over. Here again you can spend some time looking at these miracles. John records one but there are two of these and the sermon of the beatitudes is associated with them—a relatively hard and good study in itself. It is Jesus' first sermon.

My take on why he did this miracle is (1) He wanted large crowds of people to see his power. (2) His power wasn't going to be used to destroy Roman soldiers or in any other way cause physical conflict. It was going to be used to help people, feed people, heal people and show people where heaven is and how to get there. These people wouldn't have starved to death if Jesus hadn't fed them. He even made quite a bit more than they needed. Kind of like eating at grandma's house. There was always more than you needed. (3) I think God is saying my son can provide for you. This is a physical demonstration of a Spiritual law. Every good and every perfect gift cometh from above.

Verse 6:14 indicates something about what the scholars of the day thought. They were looking for someone like the Old Testament prophets. Someone they could make their king and he could do battle for them. Their desires were purely physical. They failed to see the corruption in their spiritual life. What they saw was a man that could make bread and fish and probably everything else they would need and required nothing from them. They were ready to make him their king. I want to skip over the next miracle here and look at verses 6: 25-59. It is Jesus telling why he did this miracle and all the things he did. It is to establish who he is, what God his father and ours has given him to do and establish this new covenant. I am going to insert it here. I don't believe I can say anything that will make it any clearer.

Chapter 14
†

Jesus the Bread of Life

John 6: 25-59

John 6:25 *When they found him on the other side of the lake, they asked him, "Rabbi, when did you get here?"*

26 Jesus answered, "Very truly I tell you, you are looking for me, not because you saw the signs I performed but because you ate the loaves and had your fill. 27 Do not work for food that spoils, but for food that endures to eternal life, which the Son of Man will give you. For on him God the Father has placed his seal of approval."

28 Then they asked him, "What must we do to do the works God requires?"

29 Jesus answered, "The work of God is this: to believe in the one he has sent."

30 So they asked him, "What sign then will you give that we may see it and believe you? What will you do? 31 Our ancestors ate the manna in the wilderness; as it is written: 'He gave them bread from heaven to eat.'"

32 Jesus said to them, "Very truly I tell you, it is not Moses who has given you the bread from heaven, but it is my Father who gives you bread that comes down from heaven and gives life to the world. 33 For the bread of God is the bread that comes down from heaven and gives life to the world."

34 "Sir," they said, "always give us this bread."

35 Then Jesus declared, "I am the bread of life. Whoever comes to me will never go hungry, and whoever believes in me will never be thirsty. 36 But as I told you, you have seen me and still you do not believe. 37 All those the Father gives me will come to me, and whoever comes to me I will never drive away. 38 For I have come down from heaven not to do my will but to do the will of him who sent me. 39 And this is the will of him who sent me, that I shall lose none of all those he has given me, but raise them up at the last day. 40 For my Father's will is that everyone who looks to the Son and believes in him shall have eternal life, and I will raise them up at the last day."

41 At this the Jews there began to grumble about him because he said, "I am the bread that came down from heaven."

42 They said, "Is this not Jesus, the son of Joseph, whose father and mother we know? How can he now say, 'I came down from heaven'?"

43 "Stop grumbling among yourselves," Jesus answered. 44 "No one can come to me unless the Father who sent me draws them, and I will raise them up at the last day. 45 It is written in the Prophets: 'They will all be taught by God.' Everyone who has heard the Father and learned from him comes to me. 46 No one has seen the Father except the one who is from God; only he has seen the Father. 47 Very truly I tell you, the one who believes has eternal life.

48 I am the bread of life. 49 Your ancestors ate the manna in the wilderness, yet they died. 50 But here is the bread that comes down from heaven, which anyone may eat and not die. 51 I am the living bread that came down from heaven. Whoever eats this bread will live forever. This bread is my flesh, which I will give for the life of the world."

52 Then the Jews began to argue sharply among themselves, "How can this man give us his flesh to eat?"

53 Jesus said to them, "Very truly I tell you, unless you eat the flesh of the Son of Man and drink his blood, you have no life in you. 54 Whoever eats my flesh and drinks my blood has eternal life, and I will raise them up at the last day. 55 For my flesh is real food and my blood is real drink. 56 Whoever eats my flesh and drinks my blood remains in me, and I in them. 57 Just as the living Father sent me and I live because of the Father, so the one who feeds on me will live because of me. 58 This is the bread that came down from heaven. Your ancestors ate manna and died, but whoever feeds on this bread will live forever."

59 He said this while teaching in the synagogue in Capernaum.

We can see then that this is a composite that John put together of what Jesus said about who he actually is. Two different places are mentioned here but probably included parts of other messages Jesus delivered. If you are really seeking Jesus read this several times. Read it from several translations if you have them. Write down for yourself who Jesus is. Salvation is yours by simply believing this message. Understand it is a spiritual message. When your earthly physical life is over it will no longer play a role in where you are. Where you are will depend on what you believed and what you accepted of his body and blood – his spiritual body and blood. There is no physical part to this. His death was definitely both physical and spiritual. It is the spiritual one however that provides heavenly hope. We will all die physically. We are all spiritually dead already. The only real hope we have is through a spiritual Savior and there is only one being that fills that need and it is Jesus.

Now back to walking on the water. You can read about this in 6:16-24. It is also recorded in Mat. 14:22-33 and Mk. 6:45-52.

Chapter 15
†
Jesus Walks on the Water
John 6: 16-24

John 6:16 *When evening came, his disciples went down to the lake, 17 where they got into a boat and set off across the lake for Capernaum. By now it was dark, and Jesus had not yet joined them. 18 A strong wind was blowing and the waters grew rough. 19 When they had rowed about three or four miles, they saw Jesus approaching the boat, walking on the water; and they were frightened. 20 But he said to them, "It is I; don't be afraid."*

21 Then they "were willing to take him into the boat, and immediately the boat reached the shore where they were heading. 22 The next day the crowd that had stayed on the opposite shore of the lake realized that only one boat had been there, and that Jesus had not entered it with his disciples, but that they had gone away alone.

23 Then some boats from Tiberias landed near the place where the people had eaten the bread after the Lord had given thanks. 24 Once the crowd realized that neither Jesus nor his disciples were there, they got into the boats and went to Capernaum in search of Jesus."

It seems that Jesus insisted that they leave without him. It would appear that he wanted some alone time and we know from reading that this alone time was always spent in prayer. Prayer time for him was calm time, get instruction time, rest time, and trust time. He spent most of the night while his disciples spent a miserable night fighting the wind. If you have ever tried to row a boat in the wind you can feel their frustration. Near dawn, Jesus shows up walking on the water. They have been led to the conclusion that he is a super natural man but they just didn't expect this. My opinion is that it is a way for him to demonstrate to them that he is more a Spiritual man than he is a physical one. This miracle was also specific for the men in that boat. Peter was the most affected because he wanted to participate but failed. Something for Peter and us to look back on and see how we fail when we doubt. There is an additional part of this miracle. Jesus knows that these men have been rowing all night. I can remember working all night. About dawn you can hardly function. Jesus transported them to their destination. Can you imagine being in that boat? Rowing was over. Peace was restored. Can you begin to understand this? Jesus is exactly who he says he is. He is, along with his Father and the Holy Spirit, the creator of the universe and he is a Spiritual being which trumps physical every time. We can become one with him also just by believing.

Chapter 16
†
Many Disciples Desert Jesus
John 6: 60-71

John 6:60 *On hearing it, many of his disciples said, "This is a hard teaching. Who can accept it?"*

61 Aware that his disciples were grumbling about this, Jesus said to them, "Does this offend you? 62 Then what if you see the Son of Man ascend to where he was before! 63 The Spirit gives life; the flesh counts for nothing. The words I have spoken to you—they are full of the Spirit and life. 64 Yet there are some of you who do not believe." For Jesus had known from the beginning which of them did not believe and who would betray him. 65 He went on to say, "This is why I told you that no one can come to me unless the Father has enabled them."

66 From this time many of his disciples turned back and no longer followed him.

67 "You do not want to leave too, do you?" Jesus asked the Twelve.

68 Simon Peter answered him, "Lord, to whom shall we go? You have the words of eternal life. 69 We have come to believe and to know that you are the Holy One of God."

70 Then Jesus replied, "Have I not chosen you, the Twelve? Yet one of you is a devil!" 71 (He meant Judas, the son of Simon Iscariot, who, though one of the Twelve, was later to betray him.)"

Jesus refers to the last miracle they will be exposed to. It is his ascension. This is a very important miracle. As far as man is concerned there is no longer any part of a physical Jesus. They no longer have any ability to see him physically. My feeling is that you personally cannot read this and not make a choice yourself. Will you believe or will you turn away. Many who were following turned away. Then Jesus asked his 12 if they were going to turn away. It is clear he already knows the answer. Peter again reminds me of David in the Old Testament because he really can and does mess up severely but he has the best understanding of who Jesus really is. He tells him in another passage that he only knows this because God has revealed it to him: (Matt. 16:16-17)

Simon Peter answered, "You are the Messiah, the Son of the living God."

17 Jesus replied, "Blessed are you, Simon son of Jonah, for this was not revealed to you by flesh and blood, but by my Father in heaven."

This is followed by a statement that indicates what Judas Iscariot is going to do. Two opposite reactions to Jesus. God used each one to get his Holy plan carried out. This leads us to that ever-present question. If God already had this all planned, how could these men have a choice? Physically it is an impossible thing. Spiritually, however, it can be. The really wrong conclusion that most of the world comes to is that it doesn't really matter what we choose. IT DOES MATTER even though Jesus already knows. The whole Bible says this over and over.

CHAPTER 17
†

Festival of Tabernacles

John 7: 1-52

John 7:1 *After this, Jesus went around in Galilee. He did not want to go about in Judea because the Jewish leaders there were looking for a way to kill him. 2 But when the Jewish Festival of Tabernacles was near, 3 Jesus' brothers said to him, "Leave Galilee and go to Judea, so that your disciples there may see the works you do. 4 No one who wants to become a public figure acts in secret. Since you are doing these things, show yourself to the world." 5 For even his own brothers did not believe in him.*
6 Therefore Jesus told them, "My time is not yet here; for you any time will do. 7 The world cannot hate you, but it hates me because I testify that its works are evil. 8 You go to the festival. I am not going up to this festival, because my time has not yet fully come." 9 After he had said this, he stayed in Galilee. 10 However, after his brothers had left for the festival, he went also, not publicly, but in secret. 11 Now at the festival "the Jewish leaders were watching for Jesus and asking, "Where is he?"
12 Among the crowds there was widespread whispering about him. Some said, "He is a good man." Others replied, "No, he deceives the people." 13 But no one would say anything publicly about him for fear of the leaders."
14 Not until halfway through the festival did Jesus go up to the temple courts and begin to teach. 15 The Jews there were amazed and asked, "How did this man get such learning without having been taught?"
17 Jesus answered, "Anyone who chooses to do the will of God will find out whether my teaching comes from God or whether I speak on my own. 18 Whoever speaks on their own does so to gain personal glory, but he who seeks the glory of the one who sent him is a man of truth; there is nothing false about

him. 19 Has not Moses given you the law? Yet not one of you keeps the law. Why are you trying to kill me?"

20 "You are demon-possessed," the crowd answered. "Who is trying to kill you?" 21 Jesus said to them, "I did one miracle, and you are all amazed. 22 Yet, because Moses gave you circumcision (though actually it did not come from Moses, but from the patriarchs), you circumcise a boy on the Sabbath. 23 Now if a boy can be circumcised on the Sabbath so that the law of Moses may not be broken, why are you angry with me for healing a man's whole body on the Sabbath? 24 Stop judging by mere appearances, but instead judge correctly." "

25 At that point some of the people of Jerusalem began to ask, "Isn't this the man they are trying to kill? 26 Here he is, speaking publicly, and they are not saying a word to him. Have the authorities really concluded that he is the Messiah? 27 But we know where this man is from; when the Messiah comes, no one will know where he is from."

28 Then Jesus, still teaching in the temple courts, cried out, "Yes, you know me, and you know where I am from. I am not here on my own authority, but he who sent me is true. You do not know him, 29 but I know him because I am from him and he sent me."

30 At this they tried to seize him, but no one laid a hand on him, because his hour had not yet come. 31 Still, many in the crowd believed in him. They said, "When the Messiah comes, will he perform more signs than this man?"

32 The Pharisees heard the crowd whispering such things about him. Then the chief priests and the Pharisees sent temple guards to arrest him.

33 Jesus said, "I am with you for only a short time, and then I am going to the one who sent me. 34 You will look for me, but you will not find me; and where I am, you cannot come."

35 The Jews said to one another, "Where does this man intend to go that we cannot find him? Will he go where our people live scattered among the Greeks, and teach the Greeks? 36 What did he mean when he said, 'You will look for me, but you will not find me,' and 'Where I am, you cannot come'?"

37 On the last and greatest day of the festival, Jesus stood and said in a loud voice, "Let anyone who is thirsty come to me and drink. 38 Whoever believes in me, as Scripture has said, rivers of living water will flow from within them. 39 By this he meant the Spirit, whom those who believed in him were later to receive. Up to that time the Spirit had not been given, since Jesus had not yet

been glorified.

40 On hearing his words, some of the people said, "Surely this man is the Prophet."

41 Others said, "He is the Messiah."

"Still others asked, "How can the Messiah come from Galilee?

42 Does not Scripture say that the Messiah will come from David's descendants and from Bethlehem, the town where David lived?"

43 Thus the people were divided because of Jesus.

44 Some wanted to seize him, but no one laid a hand on him.

45 Finally the temple guards went back to the chief priests and the Pharisees, who asked them, "Why didn't you bring him in?

46 No one ever spoke the way this man does," the guards replied.

47"You mean he has deceived you also?" the Pharisees retorted."

48 Have any of the rulers or of the Pharisees believed in him? 49 No! But this mob that knows nothing of the law—there is a curse on them."

50 Nicodemus, who had gone to Jesus earlier and who was one of their own number, asked, 51 "Does our law condemn a man without first hearing him to find out what he has been doing?"

52 They replied, "Are you from Galilee, too? Look into it, and you will find that a prophet does not come out of Galilee."

In the first part of Chapter 7 we see a little reaction between Jesus and his brothers (Mark mentions 4 by name and says he has some sisters). They want to give him advice. There is nothing wrong with it but Jesus only does what God wants when God wants it. Several times Jesus does thing or changes things because his time has not yet come. He finally does make the 50-mile walk and starts teaching in the Temple. Same old problem with the Sabbath and healing on it. As I read through this, I get the feeling that things are beginning to degenerate in a big way. He points out that circumcision happens on The Sabbath. Why shouldn't a healing be allowed? It is also interesting to note that the temple guards just can't see anything wrong that would lead them to the conclusion that the law was being violated. It's also interesting to note that the crowd is misinformed. They don't think anyone is trying to kill him. From other places we see they don't know he was born in the city of David exactly where the Bible says he would be. He tells them many times that God is his father but they think Joseph is. The crowd has no clue about the Spiritual Jesus. Yet they should. Look at the miracles. Look at the facts.

CHAPTER 18
†
Jesus the Light of the World
John 8: 1-11

John 8:1 *but Jesus went to the Mount of Olives.*

Chapter 8 begins with a short sentence that Jesus went to the Mount of Olives. I wandered why this little sentence is included here. Probably indicates that there is a place here where they sometimes spend the night. I guess that he went to the same place they went back to on Friday night. Verse 53 in chapter 7 says his disciples all went home. Its not clear where this is because a lot of them lived up in Galilee. It probably means they went wherever it was they stayed when they were in Jerusalem. We see him do this several times and it probably happened even more than that. He wanted to be alone. Most of them indicate that he had deep, serious communication with God the Father during these times.

John 8:2 *At dawn he appeared again in the temple courts, where all the people gathered around him, and he sat down to teach them.*

3 The teachers of the law and the Pharisees brought in a woman caught in adultery. They made her stand before the group 4 and said to Jesus, "Teacher, this woman was caught in the act of adultery. 5 In the Law Moses commanded us to stone such women. Now what do you say?" 6 They were using this question as a trap, in order to have a basis for accusing him. But Jesus bent down and started to write on the ground with his finger.

7 When they kept on questioning him, he straightened up and said to them, "Let any one of you who is without sin be the first to throw a stone at her." 8 Again, he stooped down and wrote on the ground.

9 At this, those who heard began to go away one at a time, the older ones first, until only Jesus was left, with the woman still standing there.

10 Jesus straightened up and asked her, "Woman, where are they? Has no one condemned you?"

11 "No one, sir," she said.

"Then neither do I condemn you," Jesus declared. "Go now and leave your life of sin".

He goes to the temple the next morning. They are waiting and looking for him because they have devised a trap. Actually, it was probably a trap that they had been in themselves at times. Some of them could remember a time when a girl had been in this position but it was their favorite daughter and they hadn't taken her to the temple to be tried. They had hidden her away. etc. What we know, however, is that she was guilty. We are fond of asking where the man is. I suppose it is a good question but pretty irrelevant right here. It does point out how inconsistent people are in applying the law. What we have then is the Jewish leaders standing here with a woman who has justly been accused of a death penalty related sin. I believe they thought Jesus was going to say, "Your sin is forgiven".

He had done that before. That would show that he was claiming to be God because he could forgive sins. Obviously for anyone other than Jesus they would have been right. Here again they and we are looking through physical eyes and Jesus is doing exactly what God is instructing him to do.

He squats down and begins to write with his finger in the dirt. As I prepared this, I had a little enlightenment here and I think that I know what he wrote. Jesus said several times that he is doing what he has seen the Father do. John 5:19 we have talked about that before. When did his Father write anything? One time on 2 stone tablets. My Pastor explained in one of his sermons that they were actually only 10 words. I can narrow them down to two words each in our language. I AM, NO OTHER, NO CUSS, SABBATH REST, LOVE FAMILY, NO MURDER, NO ADULTRY, NO FALSE WITNESS, NO COVET, NO STEAL. The ability to understand these and make a choice about them is what makes us in the image of God. It isn't in my opinion the only thing but it is the main thing. He actually only made us a little lower than the angels.

What Jesus actually wrote in the sand isn't revealed in the Scripture but the effect it had, is. The Religious leaders read it and were unable to take the heat. They saw something that made them guilty. Jesus said to them "he who is not guilty cast the first stone". I think God "blessed" them with the knowledge that Jesus also knew what their sins were. It actually takes someone very self-centered to not understand the significance. This law makes us all guilty. Because we are, we have no right to judge anyone but ourselves and Jesus knows. The person in the most trouble when this started left in the best position—uncondemned by Jesus. We should note that there is a reprisal – sin no more. Do you suppose she succeeded in this? My guess is not but I wouldn't be surprised if she succeeded in not committing adultery again. I actually think that sexual standards were worse then, than they are now.

CHAPTER 19
†
Dispute Over Jesus' Testimony
John 8: 12-20

John 8:12 *When Jesus spoke again to the people, he said, "I am the light of the world. Whoever follows me will never walk in darkness, but will have the light of life."*

13 The Pharisees challenged him, "Here you are, appearing as your own witness; your testimony is not valid."

14 Jesus answered, "Even if I testify on my own behalf, my testimony is valid, for I know where I came from and where I am going. But you have no idea where I come from or where I am going. 15 You judge by human standards; I pass judgment on no one. 16 But if I do judge, my decisions are true, because I am not alone. I stand with the Father, who sent me. 17 In your own Law it is written that the testimony of two witnesses is true. 18 I am one who testifies for myself; my other witness is the Father, who sent me."

19 Then they asked him, "Where is your father?"

"You do not know me or my Father," Jesus replied. "If you knew me, you would know my Father also." 20 He spoke these words while teaching in the temple courts near the place where the offerings were put. Yet no one seized him, because his hour had not yet come."

John 8:12-20 Is Jesus telling who He is. There are several "I am" statements. He says basically that the only witnesses that He needs are himself and his Father. Here again, we need to understand Spiritual rather than physical. If you believe in him it is easy to understand and very clear. If you don't believe, it is the biggest falsehood you ever heard and you have a hard time even reading it.

CHAPTER 20
†
Dispute Over Who Jesus Is
John 8: 21-30

John 8:21 *Once more Jesus said to them, "I am going away, and you will look for me, and you will die in your sin. Where I go, you cannot come."*

22 This made the Jews ask, "Will he kill himself? Is that why he says, 'Where I go, you cannot come'?"

23 But he continued, "You are from below; I am from above. You are of this world; I am not of this world. 24 I told you that you would die in your sins; if you do not believe that I am he, you will indeed die in your sins."

25 Who are you?" they asked.

"Just what I have been telling you from the beginning," Jesus replied. 26 I have much to say in judgment of you. But he who sent me is trustworthy, and what I have heard from him I tell the world."

27 They did not understand that he was telling them about his Father.

28 So Jesus said, "When you have lifted up the Son of Man, then you will know that I am he and that I do nothing on my own but speak just what the Father has taught me. 29 The one who sent me is with me; he has not left me alone, for I always do what pleases him." 30 Even as he spoke, many believed in him.

In John 21-30, he tells them several things they flat do not understand. Failure to even begin to think of him as the Messiah and God's son prevents their minds from having any real understanding of this. The same is true of us. Even those who did believe didn't have good understanding, however, until they saw how the whole thing plays' out. When they looked back it was clear. For us it is clear if we believe. "Whosoever believeth in me shall have eternal life. In my mind the one that has deep significance right here is his saying, "where I am going you cannot go". Other people have been crucified and will be crucified in the future so he obviously doesn't mean that. I believe he means that he is going to leave God's presence, God's protection for a while. He is going to die spiritually. We can't do that because we are not alive spiritually until we accept the cleansing gift of his blood. He says several times that he is the only earthly being who has ever seen God. He also lets us know in several ways that he is with God all the time. He is completely obedient to him. He is following God's plan exactly. He has never sinned, so he has never separated himself from God. No one else is qualified to do this job of being a clean sacrifice. His blood is the only blood that will work. We cannot go where he went. We cannot do what he did. We will look at this in length when we study the crucifixion. Verse 30 is interesting and good. Many believed. We dwell on the negative a lot as does the scripture but the positive is there. Heaven is going to be full of people. Are you on your way?

CHAPTER 21

†

Sin and Slavery

John 8: 31-47

John 8:31 *To the Jews who had believed him, Jesus said, "If you hold to my teaching, you are really my disciples. 32 Then you will know the truth, and the truth will set you free."*

33 They answered him, "We are Abraham's descendants and have never been slaves of anyone. How can you say that we shall be set free?" 34 Jesus replied, "Very truly I tell you, everyone who sins is a slave to sin. 35 Now a slave has no permanent place in the family, but a son belongs to it forever. 36 So if the Son sets you free, you will be free indeed. 37 I know that you are Abraham's descendants. Yet you are looking for a way to kill me, because you have no room for my word. 38 I am telling you what I have seen in the Father's presence, and you are doing what you have heard from your father."

39 Abraham is our father," they answered.

"If you were Abraham's children," said Jesus, "then you would do what Abraham did. 40 As it is, you are looking for a way to kill me, a man who has told you the truth that I heard from God. Abraham did not do such things. 41 You are doing the works of your own father."

"We are not illegitimate children," they protested. "The only Father we have is God himself."

42 Jesus said to them, "If God were your Father, you would love me, for I have come here from God. I have not come on my own; God sent me. 43 Why is my language not clear to you? Because you are unable to hear what I say. 44 You belong to your father, the devil, and you want to carry out your father's desires. He was a murderer from the beginning, not holding to the truth, for there is no truth in him. When he lies, he speaks his native language, for he is a liar and the father of lies. 45 Yet because I tell the truth, you do not believe me! 46 Can any of you prove me guilty of sin? If I am telling the truth, why don't you believe me? 47 Whoever belongs to God hears what God says. The reason you do not hear is that you do not belong to God."

The Jewish leaders here look so stupid. In fact, stupid isn't even a strong enough word. They claim they have never been a slave of any kind. How utterly stupid. Why are you looking for a Messiah if you have no need for him. Good examples are addicts. Most of which will tell you—particularly when they are under the influence—that they aren't addicted. They could quit any time they really wanted to. Every addict and I mean every one is an accomplished liar. I think they hope that if they say it enough it will become true and of course it never does. These religious leaders even seem worse than that. They didn't even have their own nation for years and were under other nation's control a lot more than they were ever free. They are under the Romans when they make this brash statement. Jesus' next statement, however, puts everyone straight, even you and me. *Verse 35 He who has sinned is a slave to sin.* My feeling here—these Jews were not only missing the target, they weren't even facing it. I am shooting at it but miss. Jesus hits it in the center. One short sentence sums up the whole picture. A spiritual life is what Jesus offers. Read through these verses several times. It will convince you that Jesus is the only way to God. Without believing in him you have no hope. If you go back and look at Abraham you see what Jesus is talking about. What the author of Hebrews says about Abraham is a help here. (Heb. 11) His faith in God is what made him great. Even faith however is a gift from God. As you read through the rest of this chapter you see that what Jesus says is just completely unacceptable to these men. It is true for us also. We may think we can sit on a fence and believe that we don't really have to make some kind of a decision because God is just too good to punish us particularly when we aren't really all that bad but it simply isn't true. It is the difference between life and death.

CHAPTER 22
†
Jesus' Claims About Himself
John 8: 48-59

John 8:48 *The Jews answered him, "Aren't we right in saying that you are a Samaritan and demon-possessed?"*

49 "I am not possessed by a demon," said Jesus, "but I honor my Father and you dishonor me. 50 I am not seeking glory for myself; but there is one who seeks it, and he is the judge. 51 Very truly I tell you, whoever obeys my word will never see death."

52 At this they exclaimed, "Now we know that you are demon-possessed! Abraham died and so did the prophets, yet you say that whoever obeys your word will never taste death. 53 Are you greater than our father Abraham? He died, and so did the prophets. Who do you think you are?"

54 Jesus replied, "If I glorify myself, my glory means nothing. My Father, whom you claim as your God, is the one who glorifies me. 55 Though you do not know him, I know him. If I said I did not, I would be a liar like you, but I do know him and obey his word. 56 Your father Abraham rejoiced at the thought of seeing my day; he saw it and was glad."

57 "You are not yet fifty years old," they said to him, "and you have seen Abraham!"

58 Very truly I tell you," Jesus answered, "before Abraham was born, I am!"

59 At this, they picked up stones to stone him, but Jesus hid himself, slipping away from the temple grounds.

In John 8:48-59, Jesus talks directly to the Jewish leaders about who he is and who they are. They say they think he is demon-possessed and a Samaritan. He calls them liars in verse 55. This is not a polite discussion. Of course, he is right and they are wrong. The thing that is very obvious is that there is a vast difference between a person who believes and one who does not. They are not unusual for unbelievers. If you choose not to believe this, you are in the same boat. On the other hand, Jesus is very blunt with them. He needs to be. He does not want any doubt about what he believes about God and himself. There is no middle road. He wants that very clear. They need to understand that if they reject him they are rejecting God. They are rejecting the very God they think is their God. They are thinking physical and he is talking Spiritual. The dialogs about Abraham and the prophets point that out. He gives them proof after proof about who he is and who is in control. The last one here is even a little comical in my mind. I don't know where you get rocks in Jerusalem. It sounds like they may have been plentiful. It says they got some somewhere. Also this isn't the first time this has happened. While they were gathering up their rocks he just disappears. Anger and self-centeredness makes for blind unintelligent, cruel, foolish decisions. The end of Jesus' earthly life is coming, but not right now. It only comes when he is ready.

CHAPTER 23
†
Jesus Heals a Man Born Blind
John 9: 1-41

John 9:1 *As he went along, he saw a man blind from birth. 2 His disciples asked him, "Rabbi, who sinned, this man or his parents, that he was born blind?"*

3 "Neither this man nor his parents sinned," said Jesus, "but this happened so that the works of God might be displayed in him. 4 As long as it is day, we must do the works of him who sent me. Night is coming, when no one can work. 5 While I am in the world, I am the light of the world."

6 After saying this, he spit on the ground, made some mud with the saliva, and put it on the man's eyes. 7 "Go," he told him, "wash in the Pool of Siloam" (this word means "Sent"). So the man went and washed, and came home seeing.

8 His neighbors and those who had formerly seen him begging asked, "Isn't this the same man who used to sit and beg?" 9 Some claimed that he was.

Others said, "No, he only looks like him."

But he himself insisted, "I am the man."

10 "How then were your eyes opened?" they asked.

11 He replied, "The man they call Jesus made some mud and put it on my eyes. He told me to go to Siloam and wash. So, I went and washed, and then I could see."

12 "Where is this man?" they asked him.

"I don't know," he said.

13 They brought to the Pharisees the man who had been blind. 14 Now the day on which Jesus had made the mud and opened the man's eyes was a Sabbath. 15 Therefore the Pharisees also asked him how he had received

his sight. "He put mud on my eyes," the man replied, "and I washed, and now I see."

16 Some of the Pharisees said, "This man is not from God, for he does not keep the Sabbath."

But others asked, "How can a sinner perform such signs?" So, they were divided.

17 Then they turned again to the blind man, "What have you to say about him? It was your eyes he opened."

The man replied, "He is a prophet."

18 They still did not believe that he had been blind and had received his sight until they sent for the man's parents. 19 "Is this your son?" they asked. "Is this the one you say was born blind? How is it that now he can see?"

20 "We know he is our son," the parents answered, "and we know he was born blind. 21 But how he can see now, or who opened his eyes, we don't know. Ask him. He is of age; he will speak for himself." 22 His parents said this because they were afraid of the Jewish leaders, who already had decided that anyone who acknowledged that Jesus was the Messiah would be put out of the synagogue. 23 That was why his parents said, "He is of age; ask him."

24 A second time they summoned the man who had been blind. "Give glory to God by telling the truth," they said. "We know this man is a sinner."

25 He replied, "Whether he is a sinner or not, I don't know. One thing I do know. I was blind but now I see!"

26 Then they asked him, "What did he do to you? How did he open your eyes?"

27 He answered, "I have told you already and you did not listen. Why do you want to hear it again? Do you want to become his disciples too?"

28 Then they hurled insults at him and said, "You are this fellow's disciple! We are disciples of Moses! 29 We know that God spoke to Moses, but as for this fellow, we don't even know where he comes from."

30 The man answered, "Now that is remarkable! You don't know where he comes from, yet he opened my eyes. 31 We know that God does not listen to sinners. He listens to the godly person who does his will. 32 Nobody has ever heard of opening the eyes of a man born blind. 33 If this man were not from God, he could do nothing."

34 To this they replied, "You were steeped in sin at birth; how dare you lecture us!" And they threw him out.

35 Jesus heard that they had thrown him out, and when he found him, he said, "Do you believe in the Son of Man?"

36 "Who is he, sir?" the man asked. "Tell me so that I may believe in him."

37 Jesus said, "You have now seen him; in fact, he is the one speaking with you."

38 Then the man said, "Lord, I believe," and he worshiped him.

39 Jesus said, "For judgment I have come into this world, so that the blind will see and those who see will become blind."

40 Some Pharisees who were with him heard him say this and asked, "What? Are we blind too?"

41 Jesus said, "If you were blind, you would not be guilty of sin; but now that you claim you can see, your guilt remains."

Chapter 9 is all about one miracle and the Jewish leaders' reaction to it. Here again they are staring at the obvious and choose not to see it. There was a man who had been born blind. This wasn't a secret. Plenty of witnesses. First thing we see is that these physically-oriented people viewed the man's blindness as a result of someone's sin. Jesus says here that this is not the case with this man. He is blind so that God's plan can be demonstrated. It doesn't clear up the issue of why people are sick, completely, but it does let us know that illness can happen that is not the result of that person's sin. We also know that nothing that ends in a bad result originates from God.

As you read this miracle it seems gross and you ask, "when did God ever do anything like this in the OT?" but then you remember the story of Naaman. God's message through Elisha was to go dip himself in the Jordan River 7 times even though he thought that the Jordan was filthy compared to the rivers back in Syria (his country). The pool of Siloam was fed from a spring outside the city. King Hezekiah built it to provide water during a siege. It also demonstrates opening the door to Jesus; being willing to do what he wants from you. Do you really believe him or are you faking it? His promise is that the Holy Spirit will come in and help you understand what is right and good and give you what you need to do that. I can tell you that in my life that has been true. We still fail sometimes. We still sin and Satan still tempts us. Satan is not God, however. He does not have the same power. I think in my own case it is the carnal man in me that causes most of the sin. This man who had never seen before is healed and he knows who healed him—the man called Jesus. Another unique thing is that Jesus finds him again. It was after an unusual conversation with the religious leaders. They, in essence, have to admit that the man was blind from birth and can now see. His parents and many other people bear witness to this. He tells the religious leaders that Jesus did the healing so he must be a prophet. They say that Jesus couldn't have done it because he is a sinner and ask again how he was healed. I just love what he told them. 30 The man answered, *"Now that is remarkable! You don't know where he comes from, yet he opened my eyes. 31 We know that God does not listen to sinners. He listens to the godly person who does his will. 32 Nobody has ever heard of opening the eyes of a man born blind. 33 If this man were not from God, he could do nothing."* Solid proof that Jesus is who he says he is. It is clear from this and the rest of this chapter that once you have heard this message there is no middle ground. You believe or you don't. "You don't" is a death sentence.

CHAPTER 24
†
The Good Shepherd
John 10: 1-42

John 10:1 *Very truly I tell you Pharisees, anyone who does not enter the sheep pen by the gate, but climbs in by some other way, is a thief and a robber. 2 The one who enters by the gate is the shepherd of the sheep. 3 The gatekeeper opens the gate for him, and the sheep listen to his voice. He calls his own sheep by name and leads them out. 4 When he has brought out all his own, he goes on ahead of them, and his sheep follow him because they know his voice. 5 But they will never follow a stranger; in fact, they will run away from him because they do not recognize a stranger's voice." 6 Jesus used this figure of speech, but the Pharisees did not understand what he was telling them.*

7 Therefore Jesus said again, "Very truly I tell you, I am the gate for the sheep. 8 All who have come before me are thieves and robbers, but the sheep have not listened to them. 9 I am the gate; whoever enters through me will be saved. They will come in and go out, and find pasture. 10 The thief comes only to steal and kill and destroy; I have come that they may have life, and have it to the full. 11 I am the good shepherd. The good shepherd lays down his life for the sheep. 12 The hired hand is not the shepherd and does not own the sheep. So when he sees the wolf coming, he abandons the sheep and runs away. Then the wolf attacks the flock and scatters it. 13 The man runs away because he is a hired hand and cares nothing for the sheep. 14 I am the good shepherd; I know my sheep and my sheep know me—15 just as the Father knows me and I know the Father—and I lay down my life for the sheep. 16 I have other sheep that are not of this sheep pen. I must bring them also. They too will listen to my voice, and there shall be one flock and one shepherd. 17 The reason my Father loves me is that I lay down my life—only to take it up again. 18 No one takes it from me but I lay it down of my own accord. I have authority to lay it down and authority to take it up again. This command I received from my Father."

19 The Jews who heard these words were again divided. 20 Many of them said, "He is demon-possessed and raving mad. Why listen to him?"

21 But others said, "These are not the sayings of a man possessed by a demon. Can a demon open the eyes of the blind?"

22 Then came the Festival of Dedication at Jerusalem. It was winter, 23 and Jesus was in the temple courts walking in Solomon's Colonnade. 24 The Jews who were there gathered around him, saying, "How long will you keep us in suspense? If you are the Messiah, tell us plainly."

25 Jesus answered, "I did tell you, but you do not believe. The works I do in my Father's name testify about me, 26 but you do not believe because you are not my sheep. 27 My sheep listen to my voice; I know them, and they follow me. 28 I give them eternal life, and they shall never perish; no one will snatch them out of my hand. 29 My Father, who has given them to me, is greater than all; no one can snatch them out of my Father's hand. 30 I and the Father are one."

31 Again his Jewish opponents picked up stones to stone him,

32 but Jesus said to them, "I have shown you many good works from the Father. For which of these do you stone me?"

33 "We are not stoning you for any good work," they replied, "but for blasphemy, because you, a mere man, claim to be God."

34 Jesus answered them, "Is it not written in your Law, 'I have said you are "gods"? 35 If he called them 'gods,' to whom the word of God came" "—and Scripture cannot be set aside— 36 what about the one whom the Father set apart as his very own and sent into the world? Why then do you accuse me of blasphemy because I said, 'I am God's Son'? 37 Do not believe me unless I do the works of my Father. 38 But if I do them, even though you do not believe me, believe the works that you may know and understand that the Father is in me, and I in the Father." 39 Again they tried to seize him, but he escaped their grasp.

40 Then Jesus went back across the Jordan to the place where John had been baptizing in the early days. There he stayed, 41 and many people came to him. They said, "Though John never performed a sign, all that John said about this man was true. 42 And in that place many believed in Jesus.

In chapter 10 we also have only one topic and another run-in with the Jewish leaders. Jesus makes this beautiful comparison to something these people are very familiar with. The comparison is with a flock of sheep and the Shepherd. He compares himself with 2 things—one is the gate and the other is the Shepherd. We can easily see how both fit and are true. He is the gate. He does provide us the way into heaven. We mostly see, however, a flock of sheep outside the gate and how they act there. This Shepherd spends all his time with the sheep. He knows all their names. He knows how each acts. When something threatens them, he is there to protect them and they want to be close to him. They know his voice and follow him when he moves. He is what makes them a flock. Verse 16 is interesting. He says he also has other flocks. I feel pretty sure he is talking about Gentile people. Have to think of Psalm 23. Without him we can do nothing. Without him the things of this world destroy us. He is one major step better than any other. He laid down his life for us. The father gave him approval to lay it down and take it up again. He throws them a curve ball in verses 33-36. He says he is God's Son and they of course don't believe that he is anything other than a man so they again try to seize him. He points out however a remote verse in Psalms 82:6 *"I said, 'You are "gods"; you are all sons of the Most High."* And they have no answer, mostly because they really don't have a good grasp on what the Psalms and Prophets really say. This psalm is simple and really not confusing. It says that we are *gods* because we are his sons. He created us. We are his. That was the situation before Adam sinned and made us all dead in trespasses and sins. The only thing that separates us from him is sin. The sad but true thing the Bible teaches is, because we are Adam's offspring, we will all sin. We don't want to believe that, but a look at ourselves reveals that sure enough—we have sinned.

CHAPTER 25
†

The Death of Lazarus

John 11: 1-44

John 11:1 *Now a man named Lazarus was sick. He was from Bethany, the village of Mary and her sister Martha. 2 (This Mary, whose brother Lazarus now lay sick, was the same one who poured perfume on the Lord and wiped his feet with her hair.) 3 So the sisters sent word to Jesus, "Lord, the one you love is sick."*

4 When he heard this, Jesus said, "This sickness will not end in death. No, it is for God's glory so that God's Son may be glorified through it."

5 Now Jesus loved Martha and her sister and Lazarus. 6 So when he heard that Lazarus was sick, he stayed where he was two more days, 7 and then he said to his disciples, "Let us go back to Judea."

8 "But Rabbi," they said, "a short while ago the Jews there tried to stone you, and yet you are going back?"

9 Jesus answered, "Are there not twelve hours of daylight? Anyone who walks in the daytime will not stumble, for they see by this world's light. 10 It is when a person walks at night that they stumble, for they have no light."

11 After he had said this, he went on to tell them, "Our friend Lazarus has fallen asleep; but I am going there to wake him up."

12 His disciples replied, "Lord, if he sleeps, he will get better."

13 Jesus had been speaking of his death, but his disciples thought he meant natural sleep.

14 So then he told them plainly, "Lazarus is dead, 15 and for your sake I am glad I was not there, so that you may believe. But let us go to him."

16 Then Thomas (also known as Didymus) said to the rest of the disciples, "Let us also go, that we may die with him.

17 On his arrival, Jesus found that Lazarus had already been in the tomb for four days. 18 Now Bethany was less than two miles from Jerusalem, 19 and many Jews had come to Martha and Mary to comfort them in the loss of their brother. 20 When Martha heard that Jesus was coming, she went out to meet him, but Mary stayed at home.

21 "Lord," Martha said to Jesus, "if you had been here, my brother would not have died. 22 But I know that even now God will give you whatever you ask."

23 Jesus said to her, "Your brother will rise again."

24 Martha answered, "I know he will rise again in the resurrection at the last day."

25 Jesus said to her, "I am the resurrection and the life. The one who believes in me will live, even though they die; 26 and whoever lives by believing in me will never die. Do you believe this?"

27 "Yes, Lord," she replied, "I believe that you are the Messiah, the Son of God, who is to come into the world."

28 After she had said this, she went back and called her sister Mary aside. "The Teacher is here," she said, "and is asking for you." 29 When Mary heard this, she got up quickly and went to him. 30 Now Jesus had not yet entered the village, but was still at the place where Martha had met him. 31 When the Jews who had been with Mary in the house, comforting her, noticed how quickly she got up and went out, they followed her, supposing she was going to the tomb to mourn there.

32 When Mary reached the place where Jesus was and saw him, she fell at his feet and said, "Lord, if you had been here, my brother would not have died."

33 When Jesus saw her weeping, and the Jews who had come along with her also weeping, he was deeply moved in spirit and troubled.

34 "Where have you laid him?" he asked.

"Come and see, Lord," they replied.

35 Jesus wept.

36 Then the Jews said, "See how he loved him!"

37 But some of them said, "Could not he who opened the eyes of the blind man have kept this man from dying?"

Jesus Raises Lazarus From the Dead

38 Jesus, once more deeply moved, came to the tomb. It was a cave with a stone laid across the entrance. 39 Take away the stone," he said.

"But, Lord," said Martha, the sister of the dead man, "by this time there is a bad odor, for he has been there four days."

40 Then Jesus said, "Did I not tell you that if you believe, you will see the glory of God?"

41 So they took away the stone. Then Jesus looked up and said, "Father, I thank you that you have heard me. 42 I knew that you always hear me, but I said this for the benefit of the people standing here, that they may believe that you sent me."

43 When he had said this, Jesus called in a loud voice, "Lazarus, come out!"

44 The dead man came out, his hands and feet wrapped with strips of linen, and a cloth around his face.

Jesus said to them, "Take off the grave clothes and let him go."

List of Miracles:
Death and resurrection of Lazarus
Water into wine
Government official's son
Healing at the pool of Bethsaida
Feeds 5000
Walks on the water
Heals a man born blind
153 large fish

If you are counting the miracles Jesus does, that most people believe John is including in his list of "proof work of Jesus" there are probably 8 and Lazarus' resurrection is number 7. It is only recorded here in John but has to be one of the most miraculous miracles of all times. We can see here that Jesus is very definitely using this resurrection to prove who he is. What we kind of overlook sometimes is that he not only raises him from the dead he lets him die on purpose. He lets him stay in the grave for 4 days on purpose. He made sure everyone knows that Lazarus isn't just sleeping. These graveyards must have been very odiferous places. People probably went back home after a while because of the smell. Mary didn't want to go there and particularly didn't want the stone moved because of the smell. To me, it points out that there isn't anything good at all about death. It is the end of life. There are no more chances to change anything. We actually do not know what is on the other side if there is such a place. We can know what we believe but we have no physical proof of anything. In this sense it is an unknown and that is why we are afraid of it. My mom and my brother-in-law both talked to me shortly before they died and they were both Christians and very apprehensive about dying. I have also had a thought, although I am not sure it even worth mentioning. There are several people Jesus raised from the dead. Lazarus was the most dramatic. In almost every case he makes this statement that they are not really dead and yet the writing indicates that they are. His own body falls in this category. My feeling is that the Spiritual over rides the physical and the result is that the physical bodies that are going to be resurrected back to the earth are Spiritually maintained. Since the spirit world is not sensitive to time these bodies aren't affected by its passing so they don't decay. No time passes for them. This kind of redefines final death as the complete absence of God. It is the ultimate result of sin. Romans 6:23. Kind of an interesting thing is that we have no comment from Lazarus. My feeling is that this is intentional. It would not add to the purpose of this event. It was very public. Many people believed because of it. There is no doubt that it happened.

CHAPTER 26
†
The Plot to Kill Jesus
John 11: 45-57

John 11:45 *Therefore many of the Jews who had come to visit Mary, and had seen what Jesus did, believed in him. 46 But some of them went to the Pharisees and told them what Jesus had done. 47 Then the chief priests and the Pharisees called a meeting of the Sanhedrin.*

What are we accomplishing?" they asked. "Here is this man performing many signs. 48 If we let him go on like this, everyone will believe in him, and then the Romans will come and take away both our temple and our nation."

49 Then one of them, named Caiaphas, who was high priest that year, spoke up, "You know nothing at all! 50 You do not realize that it is better for you that one man die for the people than that the whole nation perish."

51 He did not say this on his own, but as high priest that year he prophesied that Jesus would die for the Jewish nation,

52 and not only for that "nation but also for the scattered children of God, to bring them together and make them one.

53 So from that day on they plotted to take his life.

54 Therefore Jesus no longer moved about publicly among the people of Judea. Instead he withdrew to a region near the wilderness, to a village called Ephraim, where he stayed with his disciples.

55 When it was almost time for the Jewish Passover, many went up from the country to Jerusalem for their ceremonial cleansing before the Passover.

56 They kept looking for Jesus, and as they stood in the temple courts they asked one another, "What do you think? Isn't he coming to the festival at all?"

57 But the chief priests and the Pharisees had given orders that anyone who found out where Jesus was should report it so that they might arrest him."

The religious leaders continue to display extreme ignorance by deciding that they need to plot to kill Lazarus too. Extreme ignorance doesn't really fit either. Uncontrolled hatred that destroys rationality might work better. If you refuse to accept this message you are running the same risk, you are doing the same thing, your intelligence level is on a par with theirs but Romans 5:8 says that until you cross this physical line of death God loves you anyway. After that, there is a judgment but it isn't to decide if you are guilty or not. You and God already know that. It is to inform you of your sentence. If you want a little glimpse of this, read Matt 25. I have faith that Nicodemus is one that did believe. Verse 45 says that some did. It does point out that following the largest or most loud talking or most influential people seldom gets you to the right place but following hard facts is always right.

As I read on through this chapter, it is clear that Jesus is going to die. There are 3 reasons. The first is that it is prophesied. The second is that it is what God intends to happen. Third is it is what the Sanhedrin is intent on doing. A spiritual thing here is that even though this is God's plan it does not erase the guilt of these men. The same is true for us. Just because we are born in sin and God knows we are going to do it doesn't change our guilt. I have struggled with this. What is also clear, however, is that I have sinned. I know this. I continue to sin at times. I know this. The Bible teaches over and over that removal of this sin is necessary to have contact with God. He provides Jesus' blood for that purpose. In order for it to work in our life we have to believe it is God's plan. Truly believing means accepting it as God's plan for our lives. We stray sometimes but we want to be on his team.

CHAPTER 27
†
Jesus Anointed at Bethany
John 12: 1-11

John 12:1 *Six days before the Passover, Jesus came to Bethany, where Lazarus lived, whom Jesus had raised from the dead. 2 Here a dinner was given in Jesus' honor. Martha served, while Lazarus was among those reclining at the table with him. 3 Then Mary took about a pint of pure nard, an expensive perfume; she poured it on Jesus' feet and wiped his feet with her hair. And the house was filled with the fragrance of the perfume.*

4 But one of his disciples, Judas Iscariot, who was later to betray him, objected, 5 "Why wasn't this perfume sold and the money given to the poor? It was worth a year's wages." 6 He did not say this because he cared about the poor but because he was a thief; as keeper of the money bag, he used to help himself to what was put in.

7 "Leave her alone," Jesus replied. "It was intended that she should save this perfume for the day of my burial. 8 You will always have the poor among you, but you will not always have me."

9 Meanwhile a large crowd of Jews found out that Jesus was there and came, not only because of him but also to see Lazarus, whom he had raised from the dead. 10 So the chief priests made plans to kill Lazarus as well, 11 for on account of him many of the Jews were going over to Jesus and believing in him.

Chapter 12:1-11 tells about Jesus being anointed with a very expensive perfume. I lack understanding here—primarily of the culture. I can understand perfume being used generously. It is easy to imagine that bad odor was prevalent in all of these places. Jesus implies that Mary has some understanding of what is coming and has reacted to that. I think that this was so good and so complete that this perfume stayed with Jesus all the way to the grave. He actually says that.

CHAPTER 28
†
Riding a Donkey
John 12: 12-19

John 12:12 *The next day the great crowd that had come for the festival heard that Jesus was on his way to Jerusalem. 13 They took palm branches and went out to meet him, shouting, Hosanna! Blessed is he who comes in the name of the Lord! Blessed is the king of Israel!"*

14 Jesus found a young donkey and sat on it, as it is written:

15 Do not be afraid, Daughter Zion; see, your king is coming, seated on a donkey's colt."

16 At first his disciples did not understand all this. Only after Jesus was glorified did they realize that these things had been written about him and that these things had been done to him.

17 Now the crowd that was with him when he called Lazarus from the tomb and raised him from the dead continued to spread the word. 18 Many people, because they had heard that he had performed this sign, went out to meet him. 19 So the Pharisees said to one another, "See, this is getting us nowhere. Look how the whole world has gone after him!"

In John 12:12-19, we see Jesus riding on a young donkey into the city of Jerusalem. You can read about this in all the Gospels. The purpose is to fulfill prophecy, obviously, but also to make God's message clear. This is not a physical invasion. This is a Spiritual one. When it is over, the Temple will no longer be in play. A new covenant will be established. The new covenant will provide the final and complete salvation of man. It will have the power to cover every sin ever committed. Instead of being the blood and body of one of many animals without spot or blemish it will be the blood and body of one man without spot or blemish. This is Jesus Christ the Lamb of God who takes away the sins of the world. He will have fulfilled every prophecy.

Now seems to be a good time to look at the word *glory, glorify, glorified*. We see Jesus uses it several times in chapters 12 through 14. He says his apostles don't understand it but they will in the future. It is very important to Jesus and we see God himself use it so understanding it must be important. I recommend you start this process by reading 12 through 14 paying attention to the times *glory, glorify, glorified* is used. As a beginning thought – to *Glorify* is to do or say something that indicates the doer or speaker knows who God is. (God here meaning the complete God the Father, God the Son and God the Holy Spirit). When God or Jesus use the word it means they have or are going to demonstrate to the world who they are. This is never done in secret but is often done in a way and time to affect some very specific people. When you think this through then you see that the Bible itself is by far the most important book ever written because it glorifies God. We also realize that when we believe in Him and accept Him into our lives we are glorifying him.

The anointing with perfume was a glorification in 2 ways. Mary was demonstrating that she knew who He was and that at some level she knew what was going to happen. You say, "David—you are just making that up. How could she know?" Well I don't know how she knew or how complete her knowledge was but she heard what Jesus said. Jesus glorifies himself by saying she anointed Him for his burial. You see He knows who He is and He knows what is going to happen.

The ride into Jerusalem on a donkey is a Glorification. Jesus does it primarily to fulfill Scripture but it also points out who He is. He is the King. He is the King of Kings but a physical king he is not. The palm branches and coats, etc. are for his Glorification but the people didn't really understand what it meant to be the Messiah.

CHAPTER 29
†
Jesus Predicts His Death
John 12: 20-36

John 12:20 *Now there were some Greeks among those who went up to worship at the festival. 21 They came to Philip, who was from Bethsaida in Galilee, with a request. "Sir," they said, "we would like to see Jesus. 22 Philip went to tell Andrew; Andrew and Philip in turn told Jesus.*

23 Jesus replied, "The hour has come for the Son of Man to be glorified. 24 Very truly I tell you, unless a kernel of wheat falls to the ground and dies, it remains only a single seed. But if it dies, it produces many seeds. 25 Anyone who loves their life will lose it, while anyone who hates their life in this world will keep it for eternal life. 26 Whoever serves me must follow me; and where I am, my servant also will be. My Father will honor the one who serves me.

27 "Now my soul is troubled, and what shall I say? 'Father, save me from this hour'? No, it was for this very reason I came to this hour. 28 Father, glorify your name!"

Then a voice came from heaven, "I have glorified it, and will glorify it again."

29 The crowd that was there and heard it said it had thundered; others said an angel had spoken to him.

30 Jesus said, "This voice was for your benefit, not mine. 31 Now is the time for judgment on this world; now the prince of this world will be driven out. 32 And I, when I am lifted up from the earth, will draw all people to myself." 33 He said this to show the kind of death he was going to die.

34 The crowd spoke up, "We have heard from the Law that the Messiah will remain forever, so how can you say, 'The Son of Man must be lifted up'? Who is this 'Son of Man'?"

35 Then Jesus told them, "You are going to have the light just a little while longer. Walk while you have the light, before darkness overtakes you. Whoever walks in the dark does not know where they are going. 36 Believe in the light while you have the light, so that you may become children of light." When he had finished speaking, Jesus left and hid himself from them.

An interesting thing happens starting at John 12:20. Some Greeks want to see Jesus and they make their desire known through Philip. Jesus doesn't grant their request but talks about it being his time to be glorified. My assumption then is that to see the Greeks He would have had to change what he was doing and it would not have glorified Him. Verse 24 makes it clear that he is going to die and this is the ultimate Glorification of both Him and the Father. Verses 25 and 26 make it clear how we are to fit in the picture.

Verses 28-32 are unusual and beautiful in the extreme. Jesus expresses his dread, for lack of a better word, but then expresses his will to allow the Father to complete his plan. Jesus speaks directly to God and says, *Glorify your name.* The meaning is clear. Christ's death on the cross is going to Glorify God's name. Then God himself speaks. The disciples hear it because Jesus says that their hearing it was for their benefit. If it had been for him then they wouldn't have heard it. God's conversations with just Jesus were spiritual things not understood by the crowd. All they heard was thunder. God said " I have glorified it in the past and will do it again". You wonder, "When did God do this?" I wonder too, but believe he is referring to the two covenants or the 2 parts of one covenant he made with Abraham and his seed (which is Christ). *I will make a great nation from you and I will send a Messiah.* God is in the process of fulfilling his promise. The people, however, just heard what they thought was thunder. They really didn't understand and if we had been there I think we would have been just as blind as they were. This is a case where *hind-sight is a wonderful thing* is a very true statement.

John 12:30-33 is Jesus' statement describing what his death really at its very core is all about. I am not sure who all falls in this judgment but one thing is made clear—Satan does. He does not have the same power (he once had) after the cross. The blood takes away his power. He loses control of those who trust the blood to make them clean and Satan cannot touch them. I heard it said, and I tend to believe, that Satan and the Spirit cannot live in the same person at the same time. If you allow it, he can still drag you to hell with him but with acceptance of the blood cleansing he cannot take you there. You are not only saved—you are safe. They all seemed to understand that he is talking about being crucified when he says he is going to be lifted up. He says that when this happens it will provide an attraction for all people. It certainly has. When you understand what he did and what that means for you it brings JOY greater than any other joy.

John 12:34-35 indicate that the crowd does not understand what he is saying. They do not understand that Jesus is speaking of Spiritual things more than physical. He calls himself the Son of Man because he is first God and he is the part of God that has become the Son of Man also. If they had believed he was God become flesh they would not have had to ask who he was. Verses 35 and 36 is Jesus' telling who he is: i.e. the light of the world. I am always reminded of this in the morning when the sun comes up. What a perfect example God provides about who His Son really is. All physical life on this planet has been created by this energy source and all life on this earth right now is totally dependent on it. If it were to disappear, I doubt that we would be alive more than about 5 minutes. Spiritual life is the opposite. We don't have it till we accept the light, the gift, the Son. There is absolutely nothing you can do to make light yourself in either case. To have life you must accept the Son. The core of this book is right here. We must have light and spiritual light is by far the most important. He has given us physical light. We have a choice where Spiritual light is concerned.

CHAPTER 30
†
Belief and Unbelief
John 12: 37-50

John 12:37 *Even after Jesus had performed so many signs in their presence, they still would not believe in him. 38 This was to fulfill the word of Isaiah the prophet: "Lord, who has believed our message and to whom has the arm of the Lord been revealed?"*

39 For this reason they could not believe, because, as Isaiah says elsewhere: 40 He has blinded their eyes and hardened their hearts so they can neither see with their eyes, nor understand with their hearts, nor turn—and I would heal them."

41 Isaiah said this because he saw Jesus' glory and spoke about him.

42 Yet at the same time many even among the leaders believed in him. But because of the Pharisees they would not openly acknowledge their faith for fear they would be put out of the synagogue; 43 for they loved human praise more than praise from God."

John adds a comment of his own here. Through his eyes there is absolutely no reason to doubt who Jesus is. He points out his works several of which we have discussed here studying John's writing. But then he points out that Isaiah says it is going to happen and he quotes Isaiah 53:1 and Isaiah 6:10. He is more or less saying that because God says it is going to happen through Isaiah it has to happen. That is true. John also points out that many of the Sanhedrin did actually believe, but were afraid of the Pharisees because the ruling Pharisees had issued a rule that anyone who followed Jesus was going to be excommunicated. That was a big deal for them. Nicodemus was an exception, however, and John says there were others even among the leaders.

John 12 44 *Then Jesus cried out, "Whoever believes in me does not believe in me only, but in the one who sent me. 45 The one who looks at me is seeing the one who sent me. 46 I have come into the world as a light, so that no one who believes in me should stay in darkness."*

47 "If anyone hears my words but does not keep them, I do not judge that person. For I did not come to judge the world, but to save the world. 48 There is a judge for the one who rejects me and does not accept my words; the very words I have spoken will condemn them at the last day. 49 For I did not speak on my own, but the Father who sent me commanded me to say all that I have spoken. 50 I know that his command leads to eternal life. So whatever I say is just what the Father has told me to say."

In verse 32, we see that Jesus hid himself from them. In verse 44 we see him again, and he is doing the opposite of hiding. He is crying out. He is preaching his last public sermon. He makes 2 statements and clarifies both. The first is that if you have seen Jesus you have also seen the one who sent him. He has said it many times. God sent him. He is doing exactly what God has commissioned him to do, including saying exactly what God tells him to say. Phillip must not have been listening. Then he says he is the light in verse 46. If you didn't get this in verse 36 you cannot miss it here. His second statement is that he isn't the judge. In verse 46 he repeats what we see in John3:17; i.e. He didn't come into the world to condemn the world –HE CAME TO SAVE IT-(emphasis added). He was crying out, however, so I think *he* may have added it. He explains where the judgment comes from, however. It comes through the words of God. They have come out of his mouth but they are God's words. This judgment will happen on your last day, he says. What and when is the last day? When, I am not entirely sure about, but I am pretty sure it is your first day of eternity. It is the day you have no more days here. The what is that you face the judgment. These words and miracles and your rejection will be brought before you and you will be unclean because you don't have the cleansing blood of Christ to make you presentable to God. If you want a description of it read Matt.24 and 25. You will see that this Judgment is not like a court trial that we are used to. It isn't an effort to determine your guilt or innocence. It isn't even something to determine how bad your sin was so that the appropriate sentence can be administered. It only serves one purpose and that is to inform you of why and where you will spend eternity. Matthew describes some conversation between you and God but its only purpose is making dead sure you understand what the result of sin is. Remember, you are not reading the words of Jesus but the words of God himself. They are just coming out of the mouth of the Son of Man.

CHAPTER 31

†

Jesus Washes His Disciples' Feet

John 13: 1-17

John 13:1 *It was just before the Passover Festival. Jesus knew that the hour had come for him to leave this world and go to the Father. Having loved his own who were in the world, he loved them to the end.*
2 The evening meal was in progress, and the devil had already prompted Judas, the son of Simon Iscariot, to betray Jesus. 3 Jesus knew that the Father had put all things under his power, and that he had come from God and was returning to God; 4 so he got up from the meal, took off his outer clothing, and wrapped a towel around his waist. 5 After that, he poured water into a basin and began to wash his disciples' feet, drying them with the towel that was wrapped around him.
6 He came to Simon Peter, who said to him, "Lord, are you going to wash my feet?"
7 Jesus replied, "You do not realize now what I am doing, but later you will understand."
8 "No," said Peter, "you shall never wash my feet."
"Jesus answered, "Unless I wash you, you have no part with me."
9 "Then, Lord," Simon Peter replied, "not just my feet but my hands and my head as well!"
10 Jesus answered, "Those who have had a bath need only to wash their feet; their whole body is clean. And you are clean, though not every one of you.
11 For he knew who was going to betray him, and that was why he said not every one was clean.
12 When he had finished washing their feet, he put on his clothes and returned to his place. "Do you understand what I have done for you?" he asked them.

13 "You call me 'Teacher' and 'Lord,' and rightly so, for that is what I am. 14 Now that I, your Lord and Teacher, have washed your feet, you also should wash one another's feet. 15 I have set you an example that you should do as I have done for you. 16 Very truly I tell you, no servant is greater than his master, nor is a messenger greater than the one who sent him. 17 Now that you know these things, you will be blessed if you do them."

Chapter 13 begins with Jesus doing something that I believe really put the disciples out of their comfort zone. A place we don't normally want to be. There are times when it is good however and this is one of those times. He takes off his outer garment and gets a towel and some kind of basin and proceeds to wash 12 pairs of feet. It is interesting to note that Judas is included in this group. He says this in verse 10. Peter and Jesus have a little conversation. Peter as usual wants to run the show. Hasn't got the picture yet that Jesus doesn't make mistakes or does anything else that needs modifying. I know people like this. Some are much worse than others. We all—especially US citizens—are bad about it. We have lived in a freer society than anyone else in the world. We think we know it all. I think we all do it to some degree. Mary and Martha both had this problem. Judas had it big time. Thomas and Phillip both had it. You can read the verses and see the outcome.

Jesus then talks to them about what he has just done. After all, he is the Messiah, they think. Why would the Messiah do this? I mean, he is higher than the High Priest and the High Priest certainly isn't going to wash anyone's feet. Again he is teaching a spiritual lesson. Read the explanation he gives. The kingdom of heaven is a spiritual place. Among us redeemed sons I don't think there will be any rank. He also wants us to start here and practice with each other. Washing feet isn't the only way we can practice. Be helpful and kind in every way that you can be with every Christian Brother. Also do this with the unsaved so that they will be receptive to what you say when you tell them this story.

Jesus Predicts His Betrayal

18 "I am not referring to all of you; I know those I have chosen. But this is to fulfill this passage of Scripture: 'He who shared my bread has turned " "against me.'

19 "I am telling you now before it happens, so that when it does happen you will believe that I am who I am.

20 Very truly I tell you, whoever accepts anyone I send accepts me; and whoever accepts me accepts the one who sent me."

21 After he had said this, Jesus was troubled in spirit and testified, "Very truly I tell you, one of you is going to betray me."

22 His disciples stared at one another, at a loss to know which of them he meant. 23 One of them, the disciple whom Jesus loved, was reclining next to him. 24 Simon Peter motioned to this disciple and said, "Ask him which one he means."

25 Leaning back against Jesus, he asked him, "Lord, who is it?"

26 Jesus answered, "It is the one to whom I will give this piece of bread when I have dipped it in the dish." Then, dipping the piece of bread, he gave it to Judas, the son of Simon Iscariot.

27 As soon as Judas took the bread, Satan entered into him.

So Jesus told him "What you are about to do, do quickly." 28 But no one at the meal understood why Jesus said this to him. 29 Since Judas had charge of the money, some thought Jesus was telling him to buy what was " "needed for the festival, or to give something to the poor. 30 As soon as Judas had taken the bread, he went out. And it was night."

Verses 18-30 are about Judas's decision to betray Christ. The thing I noted this time when I read this is that Satan himself participated in this. I think this is directly related to his loss of power over men's souls. John 12:31

Satan's struggle isn't with us. It is with Jesus and Jesus is going to win. In fact he is going to win on the cross. Satan isn't God. He is as foolish as the Sanhedrin. He isn't unlimited by time. He isn't all-powerful. He isn't a creator. He does not know the future. If he did he surely wouldn't be helping get Christ crucified because it is going to destroy his power over the human race. He is I believe the stupidest of all of God's creations because the stupidest thing you can do is oppose the God that made you. He has based his every action on that. Jesus says his language is the language of lies meaning nothing he says is true. When you are exposed to things that impress you as pure evil steer clear of them. Abortion is one I can think of. Untruthfulness is another. Look in your own heart with honesty and you will see these and others – all of them covered by the 10 words on the tablets of stone. The positive side is covered in Gal. 5:22-23.

Jesus Predicts Peter's Denial

John 13 31 When he was gone, Jesus said, "Now the Son of Man is glorified and God is glorified in him. 32 If God is glorified in him, God will glorify the Son in himself, and will glorify him at once.

33 "My children, I will be with you only a little longer. You will look for me, and just as I told the Jews, so I tell you now: Where I am going, you cannot come.

34 "A new command I give you: Love one another. As I have loved you, so you must love one another.

35 By this everyone will know that you are my disciples, if you love one another."

36 Simon Peter asked him, "Lord, where are you going?"

Jesus replied, "Where I am going, you cannot follow now, but you will follow later."

37 Peter asked, "Lord, why can't I follow you now? I will lay down my life for you."

38 Then Jesus answered, "Will you really lay down your life for me? Very truly I tell you, before the rooster crows, you will disown me three times!"

In 13:34 we find the 11th commandment. *Love one another as I have loved you.* I think he knows that most of the time we don't easily succeed at this. He loves us more than we love ourselves and seldom can I claim that I love others more than I love myself. That is the goal, however. We need to practice. Jesus says that this is the way the world will know who we are – that we love one another and we do it in a way that it shows.

Jesus makes a statement that they mostly don't understand. He says he is leaving and they can't go with him. Peter as usual asks the obvious question 'where are you going?" They couldn't go with him because that wasn't God's will. It wasn't because they couldn't have been crucified. They could have been but that isn't the plan. The conversation indicates that Peter is serious. He says he is willing to die with him. We see from his later actions that he didn't intend to do this without a fight.

Also, we see Peter's worst nightmare begin here. Jesus predicts Peter's denials. This is a little hard for us to understand. We say it is part of God's plan and that is a correct thought but I just rebel against it a little bit and Peter did too – a lot.

CHAPTER 32
†
Jesus Comforts His Disciples
John 14: 1-31

John 14:1 *"Do not let your hearts be troubled. You believe in God believe also in me. 2 My Father's house has many rooms; if that were not so, would I have told you that I am going there to prepare a place for you? 3 And if I go and prepare a place for you, I will come back and take you to be with me that you also may be where I am. 4 You know the way to the place where I am going."*

5 Thomas said to him, "Lord, we don't know where you are going, so how can we know the way?"

6 Jesus answered, "I am the way and the truth and the life. No one comes to the Father except through me. 7 If you really know me, you will know my Father as well. From now on, you do know him and have seen him."

8 Philip said, "Lord, show us the Father and that will be enough for us."

9 Jesus answered: "Don't you know me, Philip, even after I have been among you such a long time? Anyone who has seen me has seen the Father. How can you say, 'Show us the Father'? 10 Don't you believe that I am in the Father, and that the Father is in me? The words I say to you I do not speak on my own authority. Rather, it is the Father, living in me, who is doing his work. 11 Believe me when I say that I am in the Father and the Father is in me; or at least believe on the evidence of the works themselves. "

I have had the first part of John 14 memorized for a long time and am continuing down the page. Jesus sees so clearly what is going to happen. The apostles don't see it at all. I think mostly because they don't want to. His thoughts are spiritual. Theirs are physical. They do not want him to be gone. They don't realize they are looking at God. Verse 11 talks about believing the evidence. I remember my pastor's series: "What do you do with the empty tomb". They have seen miracles. Many of them. John includes 7 very specific ones in the first 10 chapters. Then, after reading and studying these last chapters of John I see that some outstanding works are still to be seen and will occur in the next week of their lives. They seem to be in a class by themselves and the obvious most important miracle that has ever occurred and will ever occur is here and that is the resurrection of Christ. I want to study John thoroughly and pay particular attention to these last miracles that occur in this last week. I want to see what all the Gospels say about each of them. I thought of ranking by importance but then decided I don't know that, other than the resurrection. It seems logical to study them in the order that they occurred. I also think that every miracle Jesus did had a specific purpose or more than one. I don't think there is anything random in Jesus' life or his miracles and particularly during this last time. The first of these last miracles, however, isn't recorded in John till chapter 18 so we will study in John 14-17 first.

Verse 12 makes a statement about works. "*12Very truly I tell you, whoever believes in me will do the works I have been doing, and they will do even greater things than these, because I am going to the Father.*"

It is quite clear that if you truly believe in Jesus, the result will be that you act like him. You do the same things he does. You tell about him and what his gift to the world is. He says that we will be able to do even greater things than these he has done and the reason is that he is going to the Father. In looking back we wonder what they and us may have done that is greater than he did and the answer is that collectively we have reached a lot more people. When we are generous we have fed more than 5000 people. We have gone to most of the world. He said that the reason for this is that he is going to return to the father. I am not sure I understand how this works but I believe that to return to the father he must first be separated from him. I think both things happened while he hung on the cross. The first person his blood cleansed was himself. He had no sin himself but he was bearing ours. His blood not only cleanses us it gives us freedom and it gives us power. He also promises that whatever we ask for he will give as long as it glorifies God and we ask in his name. The *bearing fruit* instructions are pretty straightforward too.

"13 And I will do whatever you ask in my name, so that the Father may be glorified in the Son. 14 You may ask me for anything in my name, and I will do it."

When we look at this carefully we can see then that God's purpose is to glorify himself and everything we do or ask in his name he will do.

In Verses 15-21 we see Jesus teaching his disciples about the Holy Spirit. This is also pretty new to them. The trinity is pretty much a New Testament doctrine.

John 14:15 If you love me, keep my commands. 16 And I will ask the Father, and he will give you another advocate to help you and be with you forever— 17 the Spirit of truth. The world cannot accept him, because it neither sees him nor knows him. But you know him, for he lives with you and will be in you. 18 I will not leave you as orphans; I will come to you. 19 Before long, the world will not see me anymore, but you will see me. Because I live, you also will live. 20 On that day you will realize that I am in my Father, and you are in me, and I am in you. 21 Whoever has my commands and keeps them is the one who loves me. The one who loves me will be loved by my Father, and I too will love them and show myself to them."

What a wonderful thing for us post-resurrection Christians. We see that this is another gift directly from God the Father. True, Jesus is involved. He asks the father to send this Spirit. We also know that it doesn't happen right away; completely. Jesus calls him the Spirit of truth and what a beautiful thought that is. The Spirit is the direct opposite of Satan. Satan is no match for the Holy Spirit. Satan is the father if lies. He never speaks the truth and the Holy Spirit never speaks a lie. We, however, find ourselves capable of doing both. You can't do them both at the same time, however, so who do you want to be in charge of your life? If you are like me your answer is " I want to be in charge. I want to make the decisions based on my circumstances." When you bow your head and submit to God, however, you know in the core of your being which way you should go. Lying is never right. The truth is always best. The Book says "you shall know the truth and the truth shall set you free". John 8:32. Verses 20-21 also point out that if you are serious about committing yourself to Jesus you will keep his commandments. The way we prove our love is with obedience to His commands. He points out clearly that this is not optional. Read these verses several times if you must but get your head out of the sand, get your feet out of the mud, put away the idea that there is wiggle room. God, Jesus, and the Holy Spirit are one, their motivation is love, they offer eternal life as the reward for loving them. Proof of your love can only be demonstrated one way and that is obedience to their command. Their command is simple and easy to understand. Love God, Love your fellowman and Love each other as much as Jesus loves you. Death itself is better than disobedience. At the end of verse 21 he says he will show himself to them. "Them" here I believe is referring to those who believed that he was the Messiah before he was crucified. Down in verses 28 and 29 he says this.

Verse 19 indicates that unsaved people will not see his resurrected body. Also in this section we see that Love results in obedience. He states without doubt that Love results in obedience. He wants us indeed commands us to Love each other as much as He loves us. He loved us enough to die for us. Romans 5:8 says God loved us enough to sacrifice his Son and he did this while we were still sinners. This seems to me an unattainable goal. I believe it is impossible without the help of the Advocate—the Holy Spirit.

John 14:22 Then Judas (not Judas Iscariot) said, "But, Lord, why do you intend to show yourself to us and not to the world?"
23 Jesus replied, "Anyone who loves me will obey my teaching. My Father will love them, and we will come to them and make our home with them. 24 Anyone who does not love me will not obey my teaching. These words you hear are not my own; they belong to the Father who sent me."
25 "All this I have spoken while still with you. 26 But the Advocate, the Holy Spirit, whom the Father will send in my name, will teach you all things and will remind you of everything I have said to you. 27 Peace I leave with "you; my peace I give you. I do not give to you as the world gives. Do not let your hearts be troubled and do not be afraid.
28 "You heard me say, 'I am going away and I am coming back to you.' If you

loved me, you would be glad that I am going to the Father, for the Father is greater than I. 29 I have told you now before it happens, so that when it does happen you will believe. 30 I will not say much more to you, for the prince of this world is coming. He has no hold over me, 31 but he comes so that the world may learn that I love the Father and do exactly what my Father has commanded me.
"Come now; let us leave."

In verse 22 we hear Judas (not Iscariot) ask a question. At first it doesn't seem like Jesus answers the question but then we see he actually does answer in pretty serious detail. He only makes one comment about the unbelievers. You can tell who they are because they are not obeying his teaching.

Verses 25-27 are assurance verses. He knows they don't know what is really happening. He says to them that he is saying all this so that when it is all over they will understand and part of the reason is that they WILL have the Holy Spirit. In the last of 27 he says don't let your heart be troubled or afraid. Don't know of any one of them that succeeded in this. There are times like this I am sure Jesus understands but the fact is when they come he wants us to stop and pray and listen with our hearts and not be troubled and afraid. It often happens when some loved one is dying. We just need to remember that eternity is forever and for the Christian heaven is the perfect place. Verses 30-31 indicate that Satan himself was with the crowd that came to the garden. Two last thoughts in these verses—he wants us to have peace. He is in the most difficult possible situation and he says we should have peace. But then he says we should be glad that this is happening because he is going to the father and the father is greater than he. My feeling here is that he knows this is coming to a perfect conclusion. It is exactly what God wants. By evening the suffering he has to bear will be over. The price will be paid. Satan will face defeat. Sin will be paid for. Life untainted by sin will be possible for believers. The Holy Spirit will soon become the indwelling Spirit of God in the human heart – AND WILL BRING REAL PEACE. I'm not sure John 14 isn't the most important chapter in the Bible.

John 15,16 and 17 are almost all red letters in a red-letter Bible. I am not sure of the timing here because it sounds like they leave the upper room at the end of 14. It doesn't really matter. The first thing Jesus talks about in chapter 15 is a comparison of God to a farmer who owns a vineyard. He compares himself to a grape vine and us to the branches that grow the fruit. He says that if we are a branch that doesn't grow fruit the farmer removes us from the vine. We are thrown into the fire.

CHAPTER 33

✝

The Vine and the Branches
John 15: 1-27

John 15:1 *"I am the true vine, and my Father is the gardener. 2 He cuts off every branch in me that bears no fruit, while every branch that does bear fruit he prunes so that it will be even more fruitful. 3 You are already clean because of the word I have spoken to you. 4 Remain in me, as I also remain in you. No branch can bear fruit by itself; it must remain in the vine. Neither can you bear fruit unless you remain in me.*

5 "I am the vine; you are the branches. If you remain in me and I in you, you will bear much fruit; apart from me you can do nothing. 6 If you do not remain in me, you are like a branch that is thrown away and withers; such branches are picked up, thrown into the fire and burned. 7 If you remain in me and my words remain in you, ask whatever you wish, and it will be done for you.

8 This is to my Father's glory, that you bear much fruit, showing yourselves to be my friends, for everything that I learned from my Father I have made known to you.

9 "As the Father has loved me, so have I loved you. Now remain in my love. 10 If you keep my commands, you will remain in my love, just as I have kept my Father's commands and remain in his love. 11 I have told you this so that my joy may be in you and that your joy may be complete. 12 My command is this: Love each other as I have loved you. 13 Greater love has no one than this: to lay down one's life for one's friends. 14 You are my friends if you do what I command. 15 I no longer call you servants, because a servant does not know his master's business. Instead, I have called you friends, for everything that I learned from my Father I have made known to you. 16 You did not choose me, but I chose you and appointed you so that you might go and bear fruit—fruit that will last—and so that whatever you ask in my name the Father will give you. 17 This is my command: Love each other."

James teaches in a similar fashion. Sonship to God is proven by obedience. He also points out that you have to have his help and you have to be obedient to his laws. Does this mean we won't ever stumble? I sure hope not. I think a good phrase is "we are required to be intentional". He also talks about being close to him and remaining in his love. He talks about the Father loving him and he loves us as much as the Father loves him. He uses the phrase "remain in him". He repeats again that we should love each other as much as he loves us. I think we really need to improve in this area. I think I do. Loving my wife and kids as much as I love myself would be a good first step. Sometimes I even have a hard time loving myself. Part of loving ones self as a Christian is being obedient to Jesus in every little aspect of life. We can't love the carnal man. Smoking, alcohol abuse, drugs, over eating, sexual promiscuity, disobeying the speed laws, etc. fall in this category particularly when you know they harm or have the potential to harm your body. Love like his is the key to winning this battle. Verse 16 is an interesting one. He says that they didn't choose him. He rather chose them. This brings us to that point again—how can he choose these men and they still have a choice. My only answer is that it is what the Bible teaches. I am totally convinced that I often displease him because of selfishness. I am also totally convinced that when I confess he forgives. I am also totally conversed that I am on my way to heaven and when I die that is where I will go no matter what I do for the rest of my life. My intention however is to be pleasing to him. I do make an effort. Is it my effort that saves me? **Jesus' blood is what saves me! Thank you God!** The rest of this verse points out why he chose them—he chose them (and us) so that we will bear fruit. He chose us and them and he appointed them and us. He also gives us a promise, which we often stumble over. He says whatever we ask for he will give. Whoops—left a little piece out didn't I? "In Jesus' name" is in there. Understanding this is essential. What we ask for has to fall inside of what Jesus will approve of. The way we pray I don't believe is appropriate

in a lot of cases. We make several requests in a row mostly about healing people and protecting them from pain and sickness. Then we say "In Jesus' name" I ask this. We somehow think that obligates him to do what we have asked because of what this verse says. If we mean "Thy will be done" as in the model prayer then I believe we are on safe ground. I believe He wants us to pray for fruit - opportunities to share. I don't think these two things are here together by accident. Spiritual salvation is what he is really interested in. Then he includes His new command – that we love each other. A church full of discord will never win the fight. You will never win if what you think about every day is what is wrong with other Christians. If your church is going in a way that you think is displeasing to God my advice is go find yourself a church you can function in. Don't sew discord. True we are imperfect people but Love (even for imperfect people) is what God is saying here. Not just a little of it either. He wants us to love in the same way He loves. That love is what put him on the cross. These verses (12-17) are very defining verses. Serious is an understatement—critical is closer.
"

The World Hates the Disciples

18 "If the world hates you, keep in mind that it hated me first. 19 If you belonged to the world, it would love you as its own. As it is, you do not belong to the world, but I have chosen you out of the world. That is why the world hates you. 20 Remember what I told you: 'A servant is not greater than his master.' If they persecuted me, they will persecute you also. If they obeyed my teaching, they will obey yours also. 21 They will treat you this way because of my name, for they do not know the one who sent me. 22 If I had not come and spoken to them, they would not be guilty of sin; but now they have no excuse for their sin. 23 Whoever hates me hates my Father as well. 24 If I had not done among them the works no one else did, they would not be guilty of sin. As it is, they have seen, and yet they have hated both me and my Father. 25 But this is to fulfill what is written in their Law "They hated me for no reason"

He talks here about the hatred of the world towards anyone who believes in Christ not just Jewish nonbelievers – he says the world. He says that when you face this remember that who they really hate is him and if they hate him then they also hate God. Verse 24 explains what really makes them guilty. He has done mighty works among them – things no one else has ever done or will do again so they have absolutely no justification for not believing him. I believe in John's mind he is talking about the 7 miracles he has described in detail in the first 12 chapters. He also knows of many more however but these 7 are pretty unique. He also explains that if they already hate him then they certainly will hate anyone who is his follower.

I have a problem here with homosexual people. I am guilty of saying "I don't hate you. I hate the fact that you are homosexual." The one I am thinking of will no longer communicate with me. Not sure what to say here but if a person knows that something is displeasing to God and insists on doing it then it is pretty hard to not let it affect your attitude toward them. So often people try to make a gray area. It's not so bad, lots of people do this, I know the traffic signs says 75 but a cop won't even stop you unless you are going over 80. I am guilty here and my wife keeps me well informed. I can hear Jesus saying, "What did you gain?" My answer should be "I confess. I will stop doing that." If you are one of those people who think that homosexuality can be overlooked because some people are just born that way I disagree with you. I was born a liar and a thief and an all around selfish little punk. We all are born with carnal flaws in our nature. We are sons of Adam. That is why Christ had to come. This is the rationale of most homosexuals. You need to read Matt 19 and Romans 1 if you think the Bible doesn't teach against it. Is homosexuality worse than other sins? Well, according to Romans it is exceptionally bad because they have already committed the sin of worshiping things other than God, so God himself allows them to proceed down this deadly path. Verses 15:24 and 25 say again that people who don't believe Jesus hate Him and if they hate Him they hate the Father. Very clear—there is only black and white.

26 "When the Advocate comes, whom I will send to you from the Father—the Spirit of truth who goes out from the Father—he will testify about me.
27 And you also must testify, for you have been with me from the beginning."

In verses 26-27 Jesus again talks about the Holy Spirit coming. They really don't grasp this. I think it is repeated to emphasize it. Jesus is telling them before hand so that they will see in the future that God was in complete charge the whole time. He makes 2 points. The Holy Spirit is the Spirit of truth. What a profound thought. There is no falsehood in God and this is particularly manifested in the Spirit. If falsehoods come out of your mouth or are manifested in your actions then you are not allowing the spirit control of your life. I am reminded again about what my pastor has taught about the law and what it means when it says it has been done away with. He says that what the Spirit does is reverse our desires. It for us is no longer a list of things we can't do. It becomes a list of things we want to do. It is a list of what God is and how a Christian responds. You can see this very plainly if you compare the fruit of the Spirit in Gal.5:22-25 with the 10 Commandments in Exodus:20. What is the single most important thing in our lives? It is so very obvious. Love. What is God's main attribute? Love. God demonstrates his love toward us in this – that while we are still sinners Christ died for us. Rom.5:8. The first 4 commandments tell us what we can do to demonstrate our love for God. When the Spirit of truth moves into our lives we become obsessed with being obedient to these instructions. They are no longer a burden. They are a light to our path. God lives in a clean house and we want to live there too. We certainly don't want any clutter to belong to us when we are in his presence. These verses were spoken directly to the 12 and indicated how sever their rejection would be. He included the command that they be witnesses and I think it applies to us too.

CHAPTER 34
†
The Promise of the Advocate
John 16: 1-33

John 16:1 *"All this I have told you so that you will not fall away. 2 They will put you out of the synagogue; in fact, the time is coming when anyone who kills you will think they are offering a service to God. 3 They will do such things because they have not known the Father or me. 4 I have told you this, so that when their time comes you will remember that I warned you about them. I did not tell you this from the beginning because I was with you 5 but now I am going to him who sent me. None of you asks me, 'Where are you going?' 6 Rather, you are filled with grief because I have said these things. 7 But very truly I tell you, it is for your good that I am going away. Unless I go away, the Advocate will not come to you; but if I go, I will send him to you. 8 When he comes, he will prove the world to be in the wrong about sin and righteousness and judgment: 9 about sin, because people do not believe in me; 10 about righteousness, because I am going to the Father, where you can see me no longer; 11 and about judgment, because the prince of this world now stands condemned.*

12 "I have much more to say to you, more than you can now bear. 13 But when he, the Spirit of truth, comes, he will guide you into all the truth. He will not speak on his own; he will speak only what he hears, and he will tell you what is yet to come. 14 He will glorify me because it is from me that he will receive what he will make known to you. 15 All that belongs to the Father is mine. That is why I said the Spirit will receive from me what he will make known to you."

When I read this first part of chapter 16, I think of the Muslim religion. I am no real scholar of that religion but I have read a little of the Koran and I worked with Moslem men in Indonesia. I am told that this country has more Muslims in it than any other. It is like Christianity in one way. There as many different Muslim doctrinal differences as there are Christian ones. As different as Catholics are from Baptists. There were several times when the Muslim I was talking to attempted to stress how close the real Muslims and Christians are. I don't believe most Muslims believe that they should practice everything the Koran teaches. Some of the Koran has been copied from the Bible. I know enough, however, to know that there is one major difference. They do not believe that Jesus is God the Son. They believe that he is a prophet. Some go so far as to say he was the best prophet that ever lived. They believe Jesus did the miracles but Muhammad takes preference because he is the last prophet. They do not believe in the resurrection. They will tell you that they don't believe you are an infidel if you are a strong Christian. Their practice (works) however almost always gave them away. They believe lying is wrong but this only applies for other Muslims. Of course what the Koran teaches is that if you aren't a Muslim then you are an infidel. The rules for engaging an infidel are based on the premise that an infidel is inferior to them. Honesty just isn't required. They expect the same from you and it takes a while for them to understand that you are not that way. They hate to say "no" or anything negative. Isis and other radical Muslims use parts of the Koran to justify what they are doing. Other Muslims don't agree with them but they won't do anything to stop them or convict them of crimes because they are Moslems. The danger for me was in how I treated them. Treating anyone as inferior including Muslims is not what God wants.

Jesus seems vexed at his Apostles in verse 5 because no one had asked where He was going. He had already told them he was going to his father however. He was going to the one who sent him. My belief here is that Jesus is speaking primarily of Spiritual things. True he is going to die a physical death and we know he had a physical resurrection because his followers saw him with their physical eyes when he chose to let them. His new earthly body seemed to be more spiritual than physical. He walked and moved around and ate and was touchable but when he wanted to be somewhere he was just there. My firm belief is that Jesus also died spiritual death and a Spiritual resurrection. It is this Spiritual death that pays for our salvation. What is Spiritual death? It is separation from God. I believe both his separation and his reunion with God happened while he was on the cross. We will see this when we get to the verses describing Him on the cross.

Also Jesus again teaches about the Holy Spirit. He promises he will come but says that He has to go before this can happen. Kind of hidden in here is a major theological statement. Satan has been judged. The Holy Spirit being the spirit of truth has victory over him—the father of lies. We know from the teachings in the first part of Acts that tremendous Spiritual power comes with the Holy Spirit. Jesus ends this by saying whatever the Spirit teaches and brings he has received it from Him. It implies that Jesus knows what we need because he has been one of us. It is clear that we end times Christians have an advantage because of the indwelling Spirit. He states 3 things that the world doesn't get right. They don't understand about sin, they don't understand about righteousness and they don't understand about judgment. In short they don't understand the nature of God. Sin is the first issue. Sin is a violation of God's law. You have to believe first that there is a God. Then you have to believe that he has a law. Then you have to believe that if you break that law you will pay a consequence. You might think that this just isn't relevant but the Bible teaches just that. It begins by saying that we are created in God's own image. My conviction is that because we are created in his image we inherently know those things. We also know what his laws are. We know it is wrong to murder, steal, commit adultery, covet, lie (bear false witness). We know we are responsible for our parents. People who have never heard these rules still have these rules in their society. I don't think you can live without them. The world of unbelievers however don't want to live completely by this law. They only want to do it when it benefits them. They want a gray area but there are no gray areas with God. This permeates the Gospel of John. We will see it again. Righteousness is connected to it. It has to do with our attitude and standing with God. The world wants to know when something is wrong but they are hoping that they can violate it when it suits them and get away with it. The fruit of the spirit make believers have the opposite attitude. That is we realize we are sinners and we want to get as close to right as we can get. Judgment is pretty simple. It is not something coming in the future. It is here. When we sin the judgment, as we understand happens immediately. Christ is the judge. Sentencing may be delayed. He gives us time to accept the offered gift of forgiveness because he has already born our punishment. The Bible says however not to deceive yourself by thinking you can mock God. What ever you sew you will reap.

16:16 Jesus went on to say, "In a little while you will see me no more, and then after a little while you will see me."

17 At this, some of his disciples said to one another, "What does he mean by saying, 'In a little while you will see me no more, and then after a little while you will see me,' and 'Because I am going to the Father'?"

18 They kept asking, "What does he mean by 'a little while'? We don't understand what he is saying".

19 Jesus saw that they wanted to ask him about this, so he said to them, "Are you asking one another what I meant when I said, 'In a little while you will see me no more, and then after a little while you will see me'? 20 Very truly I tell you, you will weep and mourn while the world rejoices. You will grieve, but your grief will turn to joy. 21 A woman giving birth to a child has pain because her time has come; but when her baby is born she forgets the anguish because of her joy that a child is born into the world. 22 So with you: Now is your time of grief, but I will see you again and you will rejoice, and no one will take away your joy. 23 In that day you will no longer ask me anything. Very truly I tell you, my Father will give you whatever you ask in my name. 24 Until now you have not asked for anything in my name. Ask and you will receive, and your joy will be complete."

In 16:16-24 we see the disciples still without understanding about what Jesus is saying. Jesus understands this and explains to them in very clear terms what is going to happen. He doesn't use the word crucified here and I think that is because he is talking about the Spiritual time line. He also lets them know that it is not a very long time he is talking about that he will be out of their life. It is a very dark time both spiritually and physically. Verses 23 and 24 seem to indicate that we are to pray to the Father and not to Jesus. I actually think he is saying you can do both things. When he taught them to pray in "The Lord's Prayer" He taught them to pray to The

Father but here I think that He is basically saying that until this time they had never thought of him as part of the God Head and now they can and should think of him that way. My strong opinion is that we should not even segregate which personality off God we are praying to. They all hear and they respond to us as one. He doesn't have three wills. He only has one. The most important sentence if there is such a thing is this one. "Ask and you will receive, and your joy will be complete."

16:26 "In that day you will ask in my name. I am not saying that I will ask the Father on your behalf. 27 No, the Father himself loves you because you have loved me and have believed that I came from God. 28 I came from the Father and entered the world; now I am leaving the world and going back to the Father." 29 Then Jesus' disciples said, "Now you are speaking clearly and without figures of speech. 30 Now we can see that you know all things and that you do not even need to have anyone ask you questions. This makes us believe that you came from God."
31 "Do you now believe?" Jesus replied. 32 "A time is coming and in fact has come when you will be scattered, each to your own home. You will leave me all alone. Yet I am not alone, for my Father is with me. 33 I have told you these things, so that in me you may have peace. In this world you will have trouble. But take heart! I have overcome the world."

Jesus repeats his teaching again in these verses. I good teaching tool. Say it again so that it can start penetrating. This time the disciples say that they understand. He points out that they may believe but some hard times and actions that will show that they doubt are coming. He assures them again however that he is the victor and will overcome the world. The "world" here being everything that is evil in the realm of God. By this time we should understand that Jesus is the only one that can do this. We as human beings do not have the power to do this. We are incapable of controlling ourselves completely as he points out much less Satan.

CHAPTER 35
†
Jesus Prays to Be Glorified

John 17: 1-26

John 17:1 *After Jesus said this, he looked toward heaven and prayed: "Father, the hour has come. Glorify your Son, that your Son may glorify you. 2 For you granted him authority over all people that he might give eternal life to all those you have given him. 3 Now this is eternal life: that they know you, the only true God, and Jesus Christ, whom you have sent. 4 I have brought you glory on earth by finishing the work you gave me to do. 5 And now, Father, glorify me in your presence with the glory I had with you before the world began."*

In the first 5 verses of Chapter 17, we see Jesus praying and talking to God about glorification. The word glorify means to bring honor to by being obedient to the plan. They are obedient to themselves. They follow their predetermined plan. They do not sin by shying away from the plan when it requires the ultimate sacrifice. I don't normally think about God as being able to sin and maybe it wouldn't have been a sin if they had changed. After all it wasn't their fault that the human race was in the mess that it was in. A combination of man and Satan is to blame. If we let our carnal nature control our thinking we conclude that the whole thing seems unnecessary. God could just forgive us. The argument against that however is the entire bible and particularly this book of John and specifically Jesus' teachings and miracles in this book. He is glorifying his Father by being obedient and God is glorifying Jesus by sticking to his plan even though his plan requires the death of His son. We can glorify God and Jesus by accepting the gift of the blood sacrifice. It is the only thing that God will accept for the removal of our sin. If you are at this point and still doubt just listen again to what Jesus says. John14:11 ""Believe me when I say that I am in the Father and the Father is in me; or at least believe on the evidence of the works themselves." Also continue in this book because you are going to see several more unbelievable things that happen in Jesus life. They become entirely believable when you accept him for who he really is.

John 17:6"I have revealed you to those whom you gave me out of the world. They were yours; you gave them to me and they have obeyed your word. 7 Now they know that everything you have given me comes from you. 8 For I gave them the words you gave me and they accepted them. They knew with certainty that I came from you, and they believed that you sent me. 9 I pray for them. I am not praying for the world, but for those you have given me, for they are yours. 10 All I have is yours, and all you have is mine. And glory has come to me through them. 11 I will remain in the world no longer, but they are still in the world, and I am coming to you. Holy Father, protect them by the power of your name, the name you gave me, so that they may be one as we are one. 12 While I was with them, I protected them and kept them safe by that name you gave me. None has been lost except the one doomed to destruction so that Scripture would be fulfilled.

13 "I am coming to you now, but I say these things while I am still in the world, so that they may have the full measure of my joy within them. 14 I have given them your word and the world has hated them, for they are not of the world any more than I am of the world. 15 My prayer is not that you take them out of the world but that you protect them from the evil one. 16 They are not of the world, even as I am not of it. 17 Sanctify them by the truth; your word is truth.

18 As you sent me into the world, I have sent them into the world. 19 For them I sanctify myself, that they too may be truly sanctified."

John 17:6-19 is Jesus' specific prayer for his Apostles. Can you imagine being there and hearing Jesus pray this prayer for you. In the future I am sure they understand it better but just hearing it for the first time would be such a revelation into the future. I believe it applies to all believers but here he makes it very personal to his earthly person and for these 11 men.

He says in essence he is going to have the privilege of leaving the earth and they are not at least for a while. He prays for them to have protection from Satan. I believe that this prayer is answered. His crucifixion was the result of the evil found in men's hearts. He wants them to be sanctified and he is doing that. He is setting them apart from the world the same, as he is set apart from the world.

John 17:20 My prayer is not for them alone. I pray also for those who will believe in me through their message, 21 that all of them may be one Father, just as you are in me and I am in you. May they also be in us so that the world may believe that you have sent me.

22 I have given them the glory that you gave me, that they may be one as we are one— 23 I in them and you in me—so that they may be brought to complete unity. Then the world will know that you sent me and have loved them even as you have loved me. 24 "Father, I want those you have given me to be with me where I am, and to see my glory, the glory you have given me because you loved me before the creation of the world. 25 "Righteous Father, though the world does not know you, I know you, and they know that you have sent me.

26 I have made you known to them, and will continue to make you known in order that the love you have for me may be in them and that I myself may be in them."

John 17:20-26 is a prayer for all believers. If you are like me (and I suspect you are) you need to read this several times. At first I thought it wasn't saying much. I thought it was a lot like me saying to you "I will pray for you this week". Sure I am sincere but Jesus is saying quite a bit more than that. He bundles God and himself and us all up into one big package of love and fellowship and understanding and obedience. It is the blood of Jesus that holds us all together. The function of this relationship is to demonstrate to the rest of the world who God is and what he has done and can do. It does this by displaying to the world LOVE AND JOY AND PEACE AND PATIENCE AND KINDNESS, FAITHFULLNESS, GOODNESS, GENTLENESS, FAIRNESS AND SELF CONTROL. If you live within this realm you will have no need for the two tablets and the laws found there.

You will automatically follow them if you live within the fruit of the Spirit. Jesus says he wants to be right there with us all the time. He will be if the Spirit is there because after the crucifixion the 3 personalities of the Godhead are inseparable at this point and from then on. The binder of coarse is Love – God's love. It starts with God given to the world through Jesus and is implanted in us with the Holy Spirit. Instead of just being another prayer it is probably the most important prayer you will ever read.

    John begins 18 with the statement that when Jesus finished praying this prayer they departed the upper room and went to a garden they were used to going to. It seems like this might have been a place they were used to spending the night. It didn't take them long to go to sleep. They obviously didn't expect what would happen. Peter expected something because he had a sword. He may have been remembering what Jesus said in Luke 22:36 indicating that things have now changed. I am not sure what Jesus meant in Luke but this is apparent—Jesus intended for Peter to have his sword and do exactly as he did so that his plan could be carried out exactly as God had planned it.

CHAPTER 36
†
Jesus Arrested
John 18: 1-40

John 18:1 *When he had finished praying, Jesus left with his disciples and crossed the Kidron Valley. On the other side there was a garden, and he and his disciples went into it. 2 Now Judas, who betrayed him, knew the place, because Jesus had often met there with his disciples. 3 So Judas came to the garden, guiding a detachment of soldiers and some officials from the chief priests and the Pharisees. They were carrying torches, lanterns and weapons. 4 Jesus, knowing all that was going to happen to him, went out and asked them, "Who is it you want?"*
5 "Jesus of Nazareth," they replied.
"I am he," Jesus said. (And Judas the traitor was standing there with them.)
6 When Jesus said, "I am he," they drew back and fell to the ground.
7 Again he asked them, "Who is it you want?"
"Jesus of Nazareth," they said."
8 Jesus answered, "I told you that I am he. If you are looking for me, then let these men go."
9 This happened so that the words he had spoken would be fulfilled: "I have not lost one of those you gave me."
10 Then Simon Peter, who had a sword, drew it and struck the high priest's servant, cutting off his right ear. (The servant's name was Malchus.)
11 Jesus commanded Peter, "Put your sword away! Shall I not drink the cup the Father has given me?"
12 Then the detachment of soldiers with its commander and the Jewish officials arrested Jesus. They bound him 13 and brought him first to Annas, who was the father-in-law of Caiaphas, the high priest that year. 14 Caiaphas was the

one who had advised the Jewish leaders that it would be good if one man died for the people"

You might also read Matt.26:47-56, Mark 14:43-52, Luke 22:47-53. One thing I noticed that I hadn't given thought to before was that the first time they asked for him and He said "I am He", they all fell down. They had absolutely no power over him. They didn't even have power over their own bodies. They could have died right on the spot if he had continued his demonstration and I suspect most of them did die Spiritually. Rejecting Christ is Spiritual suicide. It seems incredible that they were so full of hatred that they continued on the wrong path even after they were forced to recognize they were only moving because he was allowing them to. Stupid, stupid, stupid doesn't even touch it. And we see Judas. He is the very epitome of what greed for money can do to your soul. I think the thing it does the worst is cloud your judgment. Jesus would have forgiven Judas if he had asked. Judas had heard this more than one time. He, however, decided like some people do that his sin was too great. If you find yourself here, Jesus' answer to you (as to Judas), "It would be better for you if you had not been born." Matt. 26:24. Don't misunderstand this. That statement is true of anyone who rejects the blood sacrifice that takes away the sins of the world. Was Judas' sin the worst sin that was ever committed? Probably. Was it too great to be forgiven? NO. Whosoever includes Judas. Next we see Peter and his sword. This is the first of the crucifixion/resurrection miracles I want to study. To really study these I will attempt to look at everything written the Bible about each of them.

Jesus Healed a Man's Ear by Putting it Back on His Head.

Matt 26:51-52   51 But one of the men with Jesus pulled out his sword and struck the high priest's slave, slashing off his ear. 52 "Put away your sword," Jesus told him. "Those who use the sword will die by the sword. 53 Don't you realize that I could ask my Father for thousands] of angels to protect us, and he would send them instantly? 54 But if I did, how would the Scriptures be fulfilled that describe what must happen now?"

Mark 14:47 47 But one of the men with Jesus pulled out his sword and struck the high priest's slave, slashing off his ear.
Luke 22:50-52 50 And one of them struck at the high priest's slave, slashing off his right ear
51 But Jesus said, "No more of this." And he touched the man's ear and healed him.
John 18:10-11 10 Then Simon Peter drew a sword and slashed off the right ear of Malchus, the high priest's slave.
11 But Jesus said to Peter, "Put your sword back into its sheath. Shall I not drink from the cup of suffering the Father have given me?"

The man's name is Malchus, John reveals. He is the high priest's servant. Peter had a sword in the garden and drew it while they were in the process of arresting Jesus. Jesus had exactly the opposite reaction Peter and probably everyone else expected. Question then is why did God orchestrate this incident. You can dream about this a lot if you want. Why did Peter even have a sword? Did it help Malchus or his master to believe? Does it help you believe? Don't spend undue time here and don't draw conclusions you can't verify. Bible is clear. Don't add. Don't take away. One thing we do know is that it changed Peter and that is proved by what Peter does between now and the next miracle.

18:15 "Simon Peter and another disciple were following Jesus. Because this disciple was known to the high priest, he went with Jesus into the high priest's courtyard 16 but Peter had to wait outside at the door. The other disciple, who was known to the high priest, came back, spoke to the servant girl on duty there and brought Peter in.
17 "You aren't one of this man's disciples too, are you?" she asked Peter."
"He replied, "I am not."
18 It was cold, and the servants and officials stood around a fire they had made to keep warm. Peter also was standing with them, warming himself.

The High Priest Questions Jesus

19 Meanwhile, the high priest questioned Jesus about his disciples and his teaching.

20 "I have spoken openly to the world," Jesus replied. "I always taught in synagogues or at the temple, where all the Jews come together. I said nothing in secret.

21 Why question me? Ask those who heard me. Surely they know what I said."

22 When Jesus said this, one of the officials nearby slapped him in the face. "Is this the way you answer the high priest?" he demanded.

23 "If I said something wrong," Jesus replied, "testify as to what is wrong. But if I spoke the truth, why did you strike me?"

24 Then Annas sent him bound to Caiaphas the high priest.

25 Meanwhile, Simon Peter was still standing there warming himself. So, they asked him, "You aren't one of his disciples too, are you?"

He denied it, saying, "I am not."

26 One of the high priest's servants, a relative of the man whose ear Peter had cut off, challenged him, "Didn't I see you with him in the garden?"

27 Again Peter denied it, and at that moment a rooster began to crow."

I wondered as I studied this how much of it John heard. I think he probably heard it all. Jesus said that they would all forsake him but he also said that he wouldn't lose any of them except Judas Iscariot. When you put this in spiritual context it is exactly as he says. Here however we see Peter and John inside of this courtyard where this first trial if you can call it that is taking place. Peter is there because John has made it possible. I think John is beginning to get the picture. Peter isn't however. Jesus is being humiliated and treated like a criminal and this just shouldn't happen. What he just cannot understand is why Jesus is taking it. Jesus told him but he obviously didn't listen. Uncontrolled anger leads to foolish actions. He says some things he later wishes with all his heart he could take back. The next miracle - A rooster crows exactly when Jesus wants it to.

"Matt26:31 Then Jesus told them, "This very night you will all fall away on account of me, for it is written:

'I will strike the shepherd,
And the sheep of the flock will be scattered.'

32 But after I have risen, I will go ahead of you into Galilee."

33 Peter replied, "Even if all fall away on account of you, I never will."

34 "Truly I tell you," Jesus answered, "This very night, before the rooster crows, you will disown me three times."

35 But Peter declared, "Even if I have to die with you, I will never disown you." And all the other disciples said the same.

69 Now Peter was sitting out in the courtyard, and a servant girl came to him. "You also were with Jesus of Galilee," she said.

70 But he denied it before them all. "I don't know what you're talking about," he said.

71 Then he went out to the gateway, where another servant girl saw him and said to the people there, "This fellow was with Jesus of Nazareth."

72 He denied it again, with an oath: "I don't know the man!"

73 After a little while, those standing there went up to Peter and said, "Surely you are one of them; your accent gives you away."

74 Then he began to call down curses, and he swore to them, "I don't know the man!" Immediately a rooster crowed.

75 Then Peter remembered the word Jesus had spoken: "Before the rooster crows, you will disown me three times." And he went outside and wept bitterly."

My thought is that much has happened in the hours between Peter cutting off Malchus's ear and now. Peter is totally disgusted with Jesus. Jesus has been mistreated, mistried, mocked, lied about, and slapped but he hasn't done anything and Peter knew that he could if he would. Not the way a King should act and He won't even let Peter help. Peter has demonstrated this by denying he even knows the man – 3 times and using foul language. Mark records it in a most dramatic way. Mark 14:71 says He began to call down curses and He swore to them," I don't know this man you are talking about."

Then I think about Jesus. He has taken a lot, been in front of some very important people, has been accused of a crime he is guilty of in one since and he states that. He is the King. In fact, he isn't just the King he is the King of Kings. He is being obedient and therefore is completely at ease. This is God's show and he is the star. There is Peter however that he is paying attention to because he has some things Peter needs to do but he isn't headed in the right direction to get them done. He has talked to Peter about it. Now it is time for the next step "have the rooster crow". Peter takes another turn. Have you ever been here where Peter is? Has Jesus ever pulled you up short and let you know in no uncertain terms that you are not headed down the path he wants you on? Has he ever convicted you that you are doing something that displeases him, that violates what you know in your heart is right? It may be something totally personal, it may be something that you and your spouse have decided is all right but there is really a conviction in your heart about it. It may be something with your children. I am convinced that if you are a true believer these things happen.

Often times things seem to get worse—much worse—but the next time we see Peter he is back with his brothers in Christ and he finally begins to get the picture. He sees the empty tomb and he hears Mary Magdalene say, "I have seen him". Jesus said, "Tell my disciples and Peter I will meet them in Galilee just as we planned." (Remember where Galilee is—about 50 miles away) I think much of what Jesus said (and Peter didn't want to hear) came streaming back into his head. Hope came. The race wasn't really over yet.

18 28 Then the Jewish leaders took Jesus from Caiaphas to the palace of the Roman governor. By now it was early morning, and to avoid ceremonial uncleanness they did not enter the palace, because they wanted to be able to eat the Passover. 29 So Pilate came out to them and asked, "What charges are you bringing against this man?"

30 "If he were not a criminal," they replied, "we would not have handed him over to you."

31 Pilate said, "Take him yourselves and judge him by your own law."

"But we have no right to execute anyone," they objected. 32 This took place to fulfill what Jesus had said about the kind of death he was going to die.

33 Pilate then went back inside the palace, summoned Jesus and asked him, "Are you the king of the Jews?"

34 "Is that your own idea," Jesus asked, "or did others talk to you about me?"

35 "Am I a Jew?" Pilate replied. "Your own people and chief priests handed you over to me. What is it you have done?"

36 Jesus said, "My kingdom is not of this world. If it were, my servants would fight to prevent my arrest by the Jewish leaders. But now my kingdom is from another place."

37 "You are a king, then!" said Pilate.

Jesus answered, "You say that I am a king. In fact, the reason I was born and came into the world is to testify to the truth. Everyone on the side of truth listens to me."

38 "What is truth?" retorted Pilate. With this he went out again to the Jews gathered there and said, "I find no basis for a charge against him.

39But it is your custom for me to release to you one prisoner at the time of the Passover. Do you want me to release 'the king of the Jews'?"

40 They shouted back, "No, not him! Give us Barabbas!" Now Barabbas had taken part in an uprising."

I hate to even try to say anything about Caiaphas and Pilate. They are two despicable characters. This section is mostly about Pilate. He makes some minor attempt to do what is right. My pastor says you have to understand the culture to get the right picture. He also says that there isn't anything new. I understand that civil law wasn't as fair as what we are used to but punishing an innocent man here is motivated by cowardly self-preservation. He is actually afraid of the Jewish leaders' ability to cause a riot and a serious riot was something that would probably cause him political problems. Verse 38 indicates that the current society didn't function on real evidence. His wife is an interesting person. She may very well be in heaven. She gave her husband good advice but he didn't listen. I'm a little like that sometimes. He tries to trade his way out of the situation but that doesn't work. He has Jesus whipped for no good reason. That I really don't understand. Public humiliation and pain made the crowd happy, I guess. Then he tried to wash his hands of the whole situation. What a farce!

Chapter 19 is the crucifixion of Jesus. You can also read about this in the other Gospels. It is in Matt.27: 32-66, Mark 15:21-37 and Luke 23:26-56. I recommend you take some time here and do this.

CHAPTER 37
†
Jesus Crucified
John 19: 1-42

John 19:1 *Then Pilate took Jesus and had him flogged. 2 The soldiers twisted together a crown of thorns and put it on his head. They clothed him in a purple robe 3 and went up to him again and again, saying, "Hail, king of the Jews!" And they slapped him in the face.*

4 Once more Pilate came out and said to the Jews gathered there, "Look, I am bringing him out to you to let you know that I find no basis for a charge against him."

5 When Jesus came out wearing the crown of thorns and the purple robe, Pilate said to them, "Here is the man!"

6 As soon as the chief priests and their officials saw him, they shouted, "Crucify! Crucify!"

But Pilate answered, "You take him and crucify him. As for me, I find no basis for a charge against him."

7 The Jewish leaders insisted, "We have a law, and according to that law he must die, because he claimed to be the Son of God."

8 When Pilate heard this, he was even more afraid, 9 and he went back inside the palace. "Where do you come from?" he asked Jesus, but Jesus gave him no answer. 10 "Do you refuse to speak to me?" Pilate said. "Don't you realize I have power either to free you or to crucify you?"

11 Jesus answered, "You would have no power over me if it were not given to you from above. Therefore, the one who handed me over to you is guilty of a greater sin."

12 From then on, Pilate tried to set Jesus free, but the Jewish leaders kept shouting, "If you let this man go, you are no friend of Caesar. Anyone who claims to be a king opposes Caesar."

13 When Pilate heard this, he brought Jesus out and sat down on the judge's seat at a place known as the Stone Pavement (which in Aramaic is Gabbatha). 14 It was the day of Preparation of the Passover; it was about noon.

"Here is your king," Pilate said to the Jews.

15 But they shouted, "Take him away! Take him away! Crucify him!"

"Shall I crucify your king?" Pilate asked.

"We have no king but Caesar," the chief priests answered.

16 Finally Pilate handed him over to them to be crucified."

"So, the soldiers took charge of Jesus. 17 Carrying his own cross, he went out to the place of the Skull (which in Aramaic is called Golgotha). 18 There they crucified him, and with him two others—one on each side and Jesus in the middle.

19 Pilate had a notice prepared and fastened to the cross. It read: Jesus of Nazareth, the king of the Jews. 20 Many of the Jews read this sign, for the place where Jesus was crucified was near the city, and the sign was written in Aramaic, Latin and Greek. 21 The chief priests of the Jews protested to Pilate, "Do not write 'The King of the Jews,' but that this man claimed to be king of the Jews."

22 Pilate answered, "What I have written, I have written."

23 When the soldiers crucified Jesus, they took his clothes, dividing them into four shares, one for each of them, with the undergarment remaining. This garment was seamless, woven in one piece from top to bottom.

24 "Let's not tear it," they said to one another. "Let's decide by lot who will get it." "This happened that the scripture might be fulfilled that said,

"They divided my clothes among them"

"and cast lots for my garment."

So this is what the soldiers did.

25 Near the cross of Jesus stood his mother, his mother's sister, Mary the wife of Clopas, and Mary Magdalene. 26 When Jesus saw his mother there, and the disciple whom he loved standing nearby, he said to her, "Woman, here is your son," 27 and to the disciple, "Here is your mother." From that time on, this disciple took her into his home.

The Death of Jesus

28 Later, knowing that everything had now been finished, and so that Scripture would be fulfilled, Jesus said, "I am thirsty." 29 A jar of wine vinegar was there, so they soaked a sponge in it, put the sponge on a stalk of the hyssop plant, and lifted it to Jesus' lips. 30 When he had received the drink, Jesus said, "It is finished." With that, he bowed his head and gave up his spirit.

31 Now it was the day of Preparation, and the next day was to be a special Sabbath. Because the Jewish leaders did not want the bodies left on the crosses during the Sabbath "they asked Pilate to have the legs broken and the bodies taken down. 32 The soldiers therefore came and broke the legs of the first man who had been crucified with Jesus, and then those of the other.

33 But when they came to Jesus and found that he was already dead, they did not break his legs. 34 Instead, one of the soldiers pierced Jesus' side with a spear, bringing a sudden flow of blood and water. 35 The man who saw it has given testimony, and his testimony is true. He knows that he tells the truth, and he testifies so that you also may believe. 36These things happened so that the scripture would be fulfilled: "Not one of his bones will be broken," 37 and, as another scripture says, "They will look on the one they have pierced."

The Burial of Jesus

38 Later, Joseph of Arimathea asked Pilate for the body of Jesus. Now Joseph was a disciple of Jesus, but secretly because he feared the Jewish leaders. With Pilate's permission, he came and took the body away. 39 He was accompanied by Nicodemus, the man who earlier had visited Jesus at night. Nicodemus brought a mixture of myrrh and aloes, about seventy-five pounds. 40 Taking Jesus' body, the two of them wrapped it, with the spices, in strips of linen. This was in accordance with Jewish burial customs. 41 At the place where Jesus was crucified, there was a garden, and in the garden a new tomb, in which no one had ever been laid. 42 Because it was the Jewish day of Preparation and since the tomb was nearby, they laid Jesus there.

It is a horrible incident. I am impressed with the evidence showing how horrible us humans can be. It also makes me deeply ashamed of what my sin caused. I also see Jesus' humanity and see him practicing the fruit of the Spirit even as he hangs on the cross. Jesus' care for his Mom demonstrates the 5th commandment and the commandment that he adds—*Love each other as I have loved you.* He loves this woman and feels responsible for her more than any other woman. She is also the only other person that has ever existed that does not have to take his divinity for granted.

The salvation of a thief. John doesn't include this but as I studied it I read all the gospel writings about the crucifixion and wanted to write what I felt.

(Luke 23:42-43) 39 One of the criminals hanging beside him scoffed, "So you're the Messiah, are you? Prove it by saving yourself—and us, too, while you're at it!"
40 But the other criminal protested, "Don't you fear God even when you have been sentenced to die?
41 We deserve to die for our crimes, but this man hasn't done anything wrong."
42 Then he said, "Jesus, remember me when you come into your Kingdom."
43 And Jesus replied, "I assure you, today you will be with me in paradise."

After studying this, I have come to the conclusion that I will never completely understand the Bible and will probably never completely understand these verses until Jesus takes me into Heaven or Paradise. Matt. 27:44 and Mark 15:32 both comment that both thieves ridicule him. One of those unanswered questions. I say not to dream up answers but here I say that this thief did do both. It is recorded that way. My conclusion is that he saw what was going on. He says that. Then it dawns on him what Jesus has said about himself and the truth penetrates his mind. (Nothing Jesus says returns to him void). The startling thing is how simple and straightforward this man's request was. I want to be a member of your kingdom and I ask you for that. If you remember this conversation is proceeded by him telling his fellow criminal that he doesn't have the right attitude about this. What he says is a study in its self. He understands that Jesus doesn't deserve what he is getting. The thing that really fascinates me is that he realizes that Jesus is a Spiritual King. Who would have thought that a thief on a cross would be about the first person to get the picture? Here again I think you can daydream a bunch on how this thief had gained enough Spiritual instruction and knowledge to know this much about Jesus. Don't add, don't take away. Accept it for what it is. The answer is pretty simple – The Holy Spirit!

Another interesting thing is Jesus' reply and what it reveals about what happened to him when he died and what happens to us. When Jesus said " You will be with me today in Paradise" He was saying that by the time the sun went down they would both be physically dead but would both also be in the same place and that place was Paradise. I am not sure where Paradise is. I do know it is NOT hell and since Jesus is going to be there and one of the best definitions of Heaven is where God is in control it is at least a part of heaven.

The Veil in the temple is split from top to bottom This isn't mentioned in John but it is in all the other gospels and it is a miracle so I wanted to include it here.

"Mat 27 50 And when Jesus had cried out again in a loud voice, he gave up his spirit.
51 At that moment the curtain of the temple was torn in two from top to bottom. The earth shook, the rocks split
52 and the tombs broke open. The bodies of many holy people who had died were raised to life.

I believe it is God's way of demonstrating what he means when he says the old law is done away with. This place where he has used to connect with his people will not be used for that any more. The old method of making atonement by bringing some blood into this holy place is no longer required. The records of this indicate that it happened at the same time that Jesus' blood was shed. We also know that man (the priests etc.) had not kept the old system with any regularity. In fact this was the third temple that was built and for many years the people were in captivity because of their sins and complete abandonment of what God had established for the remission of sin. The old system did not fail. Man is what failed. The most obvious thing the old system did was demonstrated how sinful man really is. We can see it happening even today. We keep turning our backs on what God has asked us to do. God has provided the Holy Spirit to help us do his will. In fact what John and indeed the rest of the bible is telling us is that without this

Holy Spirit we will fail just the same is the old covenant people did. I know I do. As I wrote this the words of a song came back to my mind. Without him I could do nothing, without him I'd surely fail – like a ship without a sail. The next miracle is the Saints. This also isn't in John. We find it in Matthew.

Resurrection of the Saints. I believe that Jesus' Spiritual resurrection was the first Spiritual resurrection that ever occurred and it happened very shortly after his side was pierced and the blood and water flowed down his side. THE PRICE WAS PAID for all sin including all the ones that were placed on Him. From noon till 3:00 he was away from his father (a description of hell is where God isn't). At around three we hear him commit himself back to God.

Luke 23:46. Jesus called out with a loud voice, "Father, into your hands I commit my spirit." When he had said this, he breathed his last.

I believe at that time his spiritual death was over and his physical death began. It also explains how He and the thief can both be in Paradise before 6:00PM. I say don't add and don't take away but I believe that his physical death only lasted about 3 hours also. It ended when the rock was rolled over the entrance to the tomb. My reason for this is that we read that his body did not decay. The reason I think his spiritual resurrection took place at 3:00 PM is because I believe his resurrection has to be the first one so it happened before these Saints came out of their tombs.

Matt.27: 53 they came out of the tombs after Jesus' resurrection and they went into the holy city and appeared to many people."

I don't believe these people or Christ was ever visible to unbelievers unless they are people who will become believers. I believe they have a physical body but it is the new version and is not always visible. It is much more Spiritual than physical. It appears when it chooses and where it chooses. Its actions are always intentional and rational. Jesus did eat and here I lack understanding because what he ate required a death (of a fish). My opinion is that we will eat. Jesus refers to Abraham's table. I think it may not be necessary for sustaining us as it is now, however. Paul writes about this in 1Cor. 15.

The Resurrection Body

1Co 15 35 But someone will ask, "How are the dead raised? With what kind of body will they come?"

36 How foolish! What you sow does not come to life unless it dies. 37 When you sow, you do not plant the body that will be, but just a seed, perhaps of wheat or of something else. 38 But God gives it a body as he has determined, and to each kind of seed he gives its own body. 39 Not all flesh is the same: People have one kind of flesh, animals have another, birds another and fish another.

40 There are also heavenly bodies and there are earthly bodies; but the splendor of the heavenly bodies is one kind, and the splendor of the earthly bodies is another. 41 The sun has one kind of splendor, the moon another and the stars another; and star differs from star in splendor.

42 So will it be with the resurrection of the dead. The body that is sown is perishable, it is raised imperishable; 43 it is sown in dishonor, it is raised in glory; it is sown in weakness, it is raised in power; 44 it is sown a natural body, it is raised a spiritual body. If there is a natural body, there is also a spiritual body.

45 So it is written: "The first man Adam became a living being"; the last Adam, a life-giving spirit. 46 The spiritual did not come first, but the natural, and after that the spiritual. 47 The first man was of the dust of the earth; the second man is of heaven. 48 As was the earthly man, so are those who are of the earth; and as is the heavenly man, so also are those who are of heaven. 49 And just as we have borne the image of the earthly man, so shall we bear the image of the heavenly man.

50 I declare to you, brothers and sisters, that flesh and blood cannot inherit the kingdom of God, nor does the perishable inherit the imperishable. 51 Listen, I tell you a mystery: We will not all sleep, but we will all be changed. 52 in a flash, in the twinkling of an eye, at the last trumpet. For the trumpet will sound, the dead will be raised imperishable, and we will be changed. 53 For the perishable must clothe itself with the imperishable, and the mortal with immortality. 54 When the perishable has been clothed with the imperishable, and the mortal with immortality, then the saying that is written will come true: "Death has been swallowed up in victory."

55 "Where, O death, is your victory? Where, O death is your sting?"

56 The sting of death is sin, and the power of sin is the law.

57 But thanks be to God! He gives us the victory through our Lord Jesus Christ.

58 Therefore, my dear brothers and sisters, stand firm. Let nothing move you. Always give yourselves fully to the work of the Lord, because you know that your labor in the Lord is not in vain.

We are like Jesus but there is a possibility that we are not equipped with both bodies at the same time as he is. He being the perfect sacrifice may be the only being with this capability. It is one of the things we don't know and I believe there isn't much point in trying to figure it out any further. There is a time here (~3 hrs.) that his physical dead body and his spiritual body are in different places

CHAPTER 38
†

The Empty Tomb
John 20: 1-31

John 20:1 *Early on the first day of the week, while it was still dark, Mary Magdalene went to the tomb and saw that the stone had been removed from the entrance. 2 So she came running to Simon Peter and the other disciple, the one Jesus loved, and said, "They have taken the Lord out of the tomb, and we don't know where they have put him!"*

3 So Peter and the other disciple started for the tomb. 4 Both were running, but the other disciple outran Peter and reached the tomb first. 5 He bent over and looked in at the strips of linen lying there but did not go in. 6 Then Simon Peter came along behind him and went straight into the tomb. He saw the strips of linen lying there, 7 as well as the cloth that had been wrapped around Jesus' head. The cloth was still lying in its place, separate from the linen. 8 Finally the other disciple, who had reached the tomb first, also went inside. He saw and believed. 9 (They still did not understand from Scripture that Jesus had to rise from the dead.) 10 Then the disciples went back to where they were staying."

When 6:00 PM or sunset comes this Crucifixion day is over. For about 36 hours nothing miraculous that we are told about happens. The Spiritual Jesus was not in the tomb. He was in Paradise. I don't believe his old physical body existed any longer. We are told it did not decay and if it were still there decay would have happened unless of course God just chose to preserve his physical body.

Acts 2:27. "Because you will not abandon me to the realm of the dead, you will not let your holy one see decay."

No one ever sees it again. This thought also indicates that his (and ours) Spiritual and physical bodies are always in the same place. At the end of this time, however, the evidence of the greatest of all miracles appeared. The tomb was empty.

Matt. 17:22-23 "22When they came together in Galilee, he said to them, "The Son of Man is going to be delivered into the hands of men.
23 They will kill him, and on the third day he will be raised to life." And the disciples were filled with grief."

And other places you can find that Jesus himself prophesies that He will be put to death and rise again on the third day. My answer is that he did just that. Don't add, don't take away. I believe both things can be true. No one saw him in the tomb on the third day. Mary Magdalene saw him first and he was standing outside. You may also ask what about when he says to Mary Magdalene when he tells her not to touch Him because he hasn't ascended to His Father yet. That is one I can't answer and can't think of a scenario, which fits, but I know there is one. I tend to believe there is a cleansing time and a reward time that we spend with Jesus before we are introduced to the Father in Heaven. Some form of this may have applied to Jesus before he was ready for the last phase of his ministry i.e. his 40 days of time on the earth in his new body teaching his apostles their last lessons.

Jon 20:11 Now Mary stood outside the tomb crying. As she wept, she bent over to look into the tomb 12 and saw two angels in white, seated where Jesus' body had been, one at the head and the other at the foot.
13 They asked her, "Woman, why are you crying?"
"They have taken my Lord away," she said, "and I don't know where they have put him."
14 At this, she turned around and saw Jesus standing there, but she did not realize that it was Jesus.
15 He asked her, "Woman, why are you crying? Who is it you are looking for?"
Thinking he was the gardener, she said, "Sir, if you have carried him away, tell me where you have put him, and I will get him."

16 Jesus said to her, "Mary."

She turned toward him and cried out in Aramaic, "Rabboni!" (Which means "Teacher").

17 Jesus said "Do not hold on to me, for I have not yet ascended to the Father. Go instead to my brothers and tell them, 'I am ascending to my Father and your Father, to my God and your God.'"

18 Mary Magdalene went to the disciples with the news: "I have seen the Lord!" And she told them that he had said these things to her."

Mary Magdalene sees Jesus. I have often thought of her in the wrong context probably because of a comment a friend made one time when we were talking about Christ and she intimated that Jesus may have been sexually involved with her. I don't believe that at all. The foundation of our faith is in part based on the fact that Jesus the man lived a sinless life and sex outside of marriage by Jesus' own words is a sin.

Mat 5 "27"You have heard that it was said, 'You shall not commit adultery.' 28 But I tell you that anyone who looks at a woman lustfully has already committed adultery with her in his heart"

My impression, however, is that she did love Him with all of her heart. He had healed her from demon possession.

Mar 16:9 When Jesus rose early on the first day of the week, he appeared first to Mary Magdalene, out of whom he had driven seven demons.

I think she loved him as much as was possible for her and that was a lot. She is mentioned in John here as one of 4 women who were at the crucifixion and close to him. He also loved her the same as he loves all of us chosen ones with the all-consuming Agape love. My belief is that he picked her to fill this place in history to prove that He loves women, He loves people possessed with demons, and he especially loves people who have been changed and return his devotion. He was very gentle with her and it appears to me she is the only person who saw him before he spiritually ascended to the Father. There is a bunch about this I don't understand. According to

Mark, she is the first person that he appeared to after his resurrection. My opinion is that there are no chance meetings where Jesus is concerned and particularly at this time so she must have a very special place in his heart. Another lesson here and other places is that if you want Jesus' attention then pay attention to him.

Angels appear at the tomb. Not sure if they move the stone or an earthquake comes and moves it. Doesn't matter. The women see them. We read about it in Matthew and Mark. Angels were usually Spiritual messengers. That's what they were here. They ask a very pointed question. *Why do you look for the living among the dead?* The question makes one believe that the heavenly realm thinks the earthly realm is pretty dense, sometimes. You are seeing it as a picture when it is really moving and alive. You are acting like life has stopped but it has just begun. You are thinking of life without Christ and he is offering you eternal unending life—Spiritual LIFE with Him.

Jesus appears to two people on the road to Emmaus. This is only found in Luke but is very interesting. It happens on the evening of resurrection day. Two followers of Jesus were on their way home. Their home was in Emmaus. This town was west of Jerusalem (not toward Galilee). One of them was named Cleopas (Simon in Greek). From their conversation we understand that they didn't yet grasp the knowledge that Jesus was actually the Messiah. They also lacked the knowledge of what the real Messiah was going to do. They really had no sense of the Spiritual realm. Jesus comes along side them and asks them about their problem and they are not allowed at this time to know who he is. He takes quite a bit of time right here quoting the Law and the Prophets. I think they were thinking about when they were taught some of these things. Probably their teacher also did not really grasp the significance of them so didn't bring it out. One of Jesus' statements, however, is that He did fulfill every prophecy ever made about the Messiah. It also indicates that some Spiritual eye-opening is necessary for us to have the really saving knowledge we need. I think it also sheds some light on the Lord's Supper. Actually, think we should practice this in our homes. The 2 times we see Jesus do it was at a planned meal, once with his apostles and once here with this family. The end of the miracle is that Jesus lets them see him and then he just disappears.

Jesus Appears to His Disciples

On the evening of that first day of the week, when the disciples were together, with the doors locked for fear of the Jewish leaders, Jesus came and stood among them and said, "Peace be with you!"
20 After he said this, he showed them his hands and side. The disciples were overjoyed when they saw the Lord.
21 Again Jesus said, "Peace be with you! As the Father has sent me, I am sending you."
22 And with that he breathed on them and said, "Receive the Holy Spirit.
23 If you forgive anyone's sins, their sins are forgiven; if you do not forgive them, they are not forgiven."

Jesus appears to His apostles, the 2 men from Emmaus and several others. (Thomas was missing) Still this same evening. If our bodies are going to be exact duplicates of his then we get a little hint of what our bodies will be like here. They will be real. We will recognize each other and if we have Jesus' understanding then we will recognize everyone – I believe we will recognize everyone we see. We will certainly recognize Jesus. Not sure we will ever be back on the old earth (it will pass away) but if we are I don't believe we will be exposed to unbelievers. I don't think they will see us and we won't see them. The exception to that might be seeing people who are given a chance and accept Christ because they see the evidence. We may even be involved in doing something supernatural to prove this just as Jesus did here. It will all be a lot clearer when we are no longer looking through dark glass. I like to note that Peter is here. Don't see any explanation of Jesus leaving this meeting. He gives them the power to forgive sins. This I don't really understand. I don't by any means believe that I can forgive someone of their sin. I believe that I am bound to forgive them in my heart if they confess and repent. Jesus will forgive and so should I but I didn't die on a cross for the remission of sin. Did he give his apostles something that the rest of us don't have? It appears to me that he did. I know that Peter and John and Paul and Phillip and Stephen and maybe others that weren't recorded did some miraculous things that don't necessarily continue to this day. Do healings still occur? I heard of one on the news just the other day in Houston. The Dr. involved confesses he has no explanation for what his X-rays are showing. A young girl (12 I think) had an X-ray of a tumor in her brain that the doctors agreed was inoperable. Their prognosis was 3 to 4 months. The next day (or it might have been 2 or 3 days but not long) the symptoms were gone and they x-rayed again and the tumor was not there. They showed these x-rays. The dad said that she was their miracle child. They had prayed, before she was born, for a child and she was born. They prayed that she could be healed, and praise God, she was. They are not like the ones Jesus did however in the frequency and the display of might power.

"***John 20 24*** *Now Thomas (also known as Didymus), one of the Twelve, was not with the disciples when Jesus came. 25 So the other disciples told him, "We have seen the Lord!"*

But he said to them, "Unless I see the nail marks in his hands and put my finger where the nails were, and put my hand into his side, I will not believe."

"26 A week later his disciples were in the house again, and Thomas was with them. Though the doors were locked, Jesus came and stood among them and said, "Peace be with you!"

27 Then he said to Thomas, "Put your finger here; see my hands. Reach out your hand and put it into my side. Stop doubting and believe."

28 Thomas said to him, "My Lord and my God!"

29 Then Jesus told him, "Because you have seen me, you have believed; blessed are those who have not seen and yet have believed."

The Purpose of John's Gospel

30 Jesus performed many other signs in the presence of his disciples, which are not recorded in this book. 31 But these are written that you may believe that Jesus is the Messiah, the Son of God, and that by believing you may have life in his name."

We don't know where Thomas has been during this time but he definitely saw Jesus crucified. We think of him as doubting Thomas but I believe he demonstrates exactly what most people would do and think. To me this is a very important meeting. It teaches us exactly what really happened. Jesus did get crucified and he was dead—very obviously dead and embalmed and buried. Now, however, his brother apostles are saying that they have seen him alive. That is just not possible. He is right. It isn't possible unless God himself is involved. It only happened once and it will never happen again. Jesus does for Thomas what he does for all of us in these last 40 days and that is prove beyond a shadow of a doubt that he is alive. He not only is alive, he will never die again physically or Spiritually. He promises us that same life after death if we believe. He certainly gave Thomas every possible reason to believe. He looked like himself and he had this big scar in his side and he had these scars in his hands and feet where the nails had been and he sounded and talked just like himself. He recognizes that Thomas now believes and he gives us who believe because of the evidence a special blessing.

John brings his writing kind of to a close in verses 30 and 31 but then he includes the final chapter.

CHAPTER 39
†
Miraculous Catch of Fish

John 21: 1-31

John 21:1 *Afterward Jesus appeared again to his disciples, by the Sea of Galilee. a It happened this way: 2 Simon Peter, Thomas (also known as Didymus), Nathanael from Cana in Galilee, the sons of Zebedee, and two other disciples were together. 3 "I'm going out to fish," Simon Peter told them, and they said, "We'll go with you." So they went out and got into the boat, but that night they caught nothing.*

4 Early in the morning, Jesus stood on the shore, but the disciples did not realize that it was Jesus.

5 He called out to them, "Friends, haven't you any fish?"

"No," they answered.

6 He said, "Throw your net on the right side of the boat and you will find some." When they did, they were unable to haul the net in because of the large number of fish.

7 Then the disciple whom Jesus loved said to Peter, "It is the Lord!" As soon as Simon Peter heard him say, "It is the Lord," he wrapped his outer garment around him (for he had taken it off) and jumped into the water. 8 The other disciples followed in the boat, towing the net full of fish, for they were not far from shore, about a hundred yards. 9 When they landed, they saw a fire of burning coals there with fish on it, and some bread.

10 Jesus said to them, "Bring some of the fish you have just caught." 11 So Simon Peter climbed back into the boat and dragged the net ashore. It was full of large fish, 153, but even with so many the net was not torn. 12 Jesus said to them, "Come and have breakfast." None of the disciples dared ask him, "Who are you?" They knew it was the Lord. 13 Jesus came, took the bread and gave it to them, and did the same with the fish. 14 This was now the third time Jesus appeared to his disciples after he was raised from the dead.

15 When they had finished eating, Jesus said to Simon Peter, "Simon son of John, do you love me more than these "Yes, Lord," he said, "you know that I love you."

Jesus said, "Feed my lambs."

16 Again Jesus said, "Simon son of John, do you love me?"

He answered, "Yes, Lord, you know that I love you."

"Jesus said, "Take care of my sheep."

17 The third time he said to him, "Simon son of John, do you love me?"

Peter was hurt because Jesus asked him the third time, "Do you love me?" He said, "Lord, you know all things; you know that I love you."

Jesus said, "Feed my sheep.

18 Very truly I tell you, when you were younger you dressed yourself and went where you wanted; but when you are old you will stretch out your hands, and someone else will dress you and lead you where you do not want to go."

19 Jesus said this to indicate the kind of death by which Peter would glorify God. Then he said to him, "Follow me!"

20 Peter turned and saw that the disciple whom Jesus loved was following them. (This was the one who had leaned back against Jesus at the supper and had said, "Lord, who is going to betray you?")

21 When Peter saw him, he asked, "Lord, what about him?"

22 Jesus answered, "If I want him to remain alive until I return, what is that to you? You must follow me "

23 Because of this, the rumor spread among the believers that this disciple would not die. But Jesus did not say that he would not die; he only said, "If I want him to remain alive until I return, what is that to you?"

24 This is the disciple who testifies to these things and who wrote them down. We know that his testimony is true.

25 Jesus did many other things as well. If every one of them were written down, I suppose that even the whole world would not have room for the books that would be written."

One amazing fishing trip. This is an amazing story and is only found in John. It is also unique in that it looks like John finished his writing – wrote his conclusion and then added this last chapter. There are 7 of Jesus' Apostles here. We know 5 of their names. Peter is the Person He deals with the most. It actually involves 2 miracles. One is that they caught a very large number of fish—way more than they usually caught at one time and second is that their net didn't break. 153 large fish. You can read it for yourself John 21. What is to be learned here—probably more than I have yet learned but here are some of the things I see. Jesus is in charge. He is in charge of how many fish we catch—none - if that is what he wants. More even than we asked for if that is what he wants. Obedience is required even in the little things. We may start wrong but he will guide. We will be very conscious of his presence. We will be completely and totally successful if we use his measuring stick. There are no failures, no imperfections, and no lack of necessities. I also think that it is clear that God expects us to function as people. What I mean is that he generally doesn't expect us to rely on other people to feed and clothe us while we stand up and preach his word in order for people to hear. I'm sure this is good in some cases but generally I don't think it presents the world with the right picture. Our main job is to tell the world about him. He will take care of us in every way. We will have trials but he will provide. In the second part where Peter is instructed to feed Jesus' sheep we learn about repentance. He is in charge at that time also. If he isn't, we won't get it right. We by ourselves are even incapable of repenting in the right way. Peter was upset because Jesus asked him the same pointed question 3 times. Peter in retrospect probably realized that he got asked 3 times because he sinned in the same manner 3 times and he needed to repent 3 times. I know what the Model prayer says but I am convinced here and because Jesus has convicted me about this that when we have a known blatant sin in our lives, we have to confess it by name and repent (turn away from it) if we expect to get forgiven. In my case there is also often some conviction that a corrective action needs to follow and if I won't be obedient, I become doubly guilty. Good example - you have spoken too harshly to someone. Guess what - you have to apologize. I can tell you it sure helps you avoid it in in the future. For Peter it was a tremendous restoration. A time of learning followed and Jesus was very straight with him. A life without trials was not in store. He was still partly on the wrong page. He still didn't recognize that the future of Judaism wasn't what he thought it was going to be—or at least not in his timeframe and not in this physical realm. He did change however and he did understand the tasks he was given to do. This is very evident in the first part of Acts when the Holy Spirit came down in great abundance and Peter the Evangelist stood up and fished for Men and caught about 3000. All of Jesus' miracles have lessons for all of us but I believe that this one is very specific to these 7 men. He wanted them to understand that HE IS IN CHARGE OF EVERY DETAIL OF OUR LIFE. He will never leave them or leave them unattended. The lesson is DO NOT BE AFRAID.

As an aside note, if you are really interested in making a thorough study of this then I believe you will see the need to go back and read all 4 of the gospels and the first 12 chapters of Acts. Your read through at this point may be to see everything you can about Jesus and Peter. Jesus spent more time teaching Peter than he did anyone else. Peter is around most if not all the time. He was usually the one who verbalized the questions. He is the example of what makes me make this observation: "If you want Jesus to pay close attention to you then pay close attention to Him. Talk to him. Don't worry about how you sound or whether your question is one he cares about. HE CARES. Listen carefully to your Spiritual feelings."

A comment about your Spiritual feelings. They have value and you should have them. Can you trust them completely? The answer is yes IF you are in tune with the Holy Spirit. The foundation for your and my belief system is the Holy Spirit. In my case the Holy Spirit uses the Holy Bible at least 99% of the time to give an answer. I like Bro David's comment, "There isn't really anything new, morally. Our moral code is the same as Adam's was".

Jesus' Ascension Into Heaven

Not very much is written about the remaining days in the 40-day period that Jesus remained on the earth. He did give them the great commission. We find this in Matt. 28:19-20, a short version in Mark 16:15, Luke writes it in Acts1: 8. In Acts it is immediately followed by a description of Christ's ascension.

"Act 1 7 He said to them: "It is not for you to know the times or dates the Father has set by his own authority."

8 But you will receive power when the Holy Spirit comes on you; and you will be my witnesses in Jerusalem, and in all Judea and Samaria, and to the ends of the earth."

9 After he said this, he was taken up before their very eyes, and a cloud hid him from their sight.

10 They were looking intently up into the sky as he was going, when suddenly two men dressed in white stood beside them.

11 "Men of Galilee," they said, "why do you stand here looking into the sky? This same Jesus, who has been taken from you into heaven, will come back in the same way you have seen him go into heaven."

Two angels are involved. Actually, I guess this could be two resurrected Saints but most scholars think they are angels. Two angles were in the tomb at one point when the women looked in. This is Luke writing both times and he calls them men in glowing white robes – as bright as lightening (probably hard to look at).

Jesus goes up—disappears into the clouds. What is to be learned here? It is the last time they see Jesus with their earthly eyes. His work is done. They and we are given a job. A new age begins. The age of grace. The time of the manifestation of the Holy Spirit. That is what the last 40 days and the first part of Acts is about. Christians in general can expect to be persecuted. Physically Heaven is somewhere above us. Jesus went up. In Revelation John went up. Is heaven just a spiritual place? I don't think so. What are some of the things we do know? There will be both a new heaven and a new earth. By inference the same old hell will do. How much is physical and how much is Spiritual – I don't know. Christ is the Savior of both. God is a Spirit. He has created a lot of physical things however. We tend to think almost all physical. My opinion is that in the new heaven and the new earth we will have few if any physical limitations. Will free will end? I sure hope so. One of the things I look forward the very most is the position of not being able to get myself in trouble.

This is the end of this study. We know that the Apostles and a few other men continued to perform miracles but in general the age of lesson giving miracles was over. My conclusion is (I believe that my pastor said this) the time for miracles having as their purpose to prove who Jesus is, is almost over. We see a few more in Acts and in Paul's life but they still all have the function of proving who Jesus is. I think a few may still happen but generally life goes on. If we won't believe in him after reading these well-documented incidents, and there were many, then we are not going to believe even if we see a current miracle. Jesus himself made a point like this in his parable about Lazarus and the rich man. I pray that if you are not a believer you will change your mind and believe that Jesus was real and that he died and 3 days later God brought him back to life. That is really all you have to do. It is true that if you do your life will change but first things first – BELIEVE.

About the Author
†

I really don't want to say much about myself. This is my first attempt to write and I have really been blessed by doing it. Many days I would sit 5 or 6 hours, only quitting when it was hard to see. I am relatively old and find myself with time to do this. I also think that I have been blessed by living in the most abundant time in history. Food has been abundant, work has been plentiful and rewarding, education is available, inventions have been phenomenal, and travel has been abundant. Life in general has been good. Religion has been free, at least in our country. Both my wife and I grew up in Christian homes so we lived with love and joy and peace and patience and kindness and gentleness and self-control. I am also a veteran—in my case I benefitted from that. I learned some valuable lessons you just don't learn any other way. I guess the downside I see is that war has also been plentiful.

I hope my motive is obvious. If you don't know who Jesus is, I want you to. The book " Gospel of John" in the Bible is by far the most important document you will ever read.

Made in the USA
Monee, IL
12 June 2022

97884503R00104